FAST LIVING

REMEMBERING THE REAL GARY HOLTON

TEDDIE DAHLIN

FAST LIVING

Other titles by the author

A Vicious Love Story : Remembering the Real Sid Vicious

Access All Areas

Project Polina

FAST LIVING

First Edition

Published 2013

NEW HAVEN PUBLISHING LTD
newhavenpublishing@gmail.com

The rights of Teddie Dahlin, as the author of this work have been asserted in accordance with Copyrights, Designs and Patents Act 1988.

All rights reserved. No part of this book may be re-printed or reproduced or utilised in any form or by any electronic, mechanical or other means, now unknown or hereafter invented, including photocopying, and recording, or in any information storage or retrieval system, without the written permission of the author and publisher.
Fast Living © Teddie Dahlin

Editor: Catherine
Front & back cover photo © Keith Boyce

Cover design © Peter Cunliffe
pcunliffe@blueyonder.co.uk

Copyright © 2012 Teddie Dahlin
All rights reserved
ISBN:
ISBN-978-0-9575170-1-1

FAST LIVING

TABLE OF CONTENTS

Chapter 1	First Impressions	7
Chapter 2	Who is Gary Holton?	21
Chapter 3	Heavy Metal Kids Part One	32
Chapter 4	London Music Scene	71
Chapter 5	Heavy Metal Kids Part Two	81
Chapter 6	What Gary Did Next	127
Chapter 7	From Lipservice to Holton/Steel	137
Chapter 8	Fame and Fortune	168
Chapter 9	The Final Curtain	192

FAST LIVING

**In memory of
Gary Frederick Holton**

FAST LIVING

Chapter 1

First Impressions

I remember well the first time I met Gary Holton. It was in the early spring of 1980 at a disco in Trondheim, Norway. It makes me smile when I think back to our first meeting, because Gary made a bit of a fool of himself in a cheeky, non-offensive way, of course. I was asked to go to the disco by a friend of mine—Casino Steel, songwriter, keyboard player and founding member of the London-based punk band The Boys. He had recently moved back to Norway from London and had a friend with him, whom he wanted me to meet. They had been in the studio, recording for several days, and felt they needed to have some fun.

I met Casino Steel a few years earlier, indirectly via Sid Vicious, Sex Pistols bassist. I was only sixteen years old when Sid and I fell in love. Sid was twenty and much more immature than I was, but it somehow worked—well, for a few days. He was my first love, and it was very intense and real at the time, although I knew the relationship was doomed, even at the beginning.

I worked as the translator for the Sex Pistols' Scandinavian tour in 1977, and Sid and I just clicked. When he left Scandinavia, there was no way I could get to London to see him. Malcolm McLaren (Pistols' manager) had organised another Scandinavian tour to take place straight after the US tour of 1978, but that was cancelled after the Sex Pistols famously split up. Casino was living in London at the time, and his Norwegian friends used to bring me messages from Sid when they visited him there. I didn't have a phone at home at the time, and Sid was living in a squat in Maida Vale, so we had difficulty communicating. My mother had taken my passport and any money I had, so I was pretty much stuck in Norway. I met Casino briefly just after Christmas 1977, when he visited his family in Norway, and we had a long talk about my brief relationship with Sid, but that's another book altogether.

> **"Up in Maida Vale, we were The Boys, The Clash, The Damned, and a few others. And Sid Vicious moved up to Maida Vale…"**

CASINO STEEL : I got to know Lemmy (Kilmister, Motorhead) in 1974 or 1975. Lemmy used to hang out at the St Moritz Bar, which was across the road from the Marquee Club. Lemmy was always on the fruit machine. That place was open after the Marquee Club closed. I got to know Sid in the mid-seventies. He used to hang around The Sex Pistols. He was a member of the 'Bromley Contingent'. We were up in Maida Vale in North London. The Pistols, Siouxsie and the Banshees, and Generation X were down in South London. Up in Maida Vale, we were The Boys, The Clash, The Damned, and a few others. And Sid Vicious moved up to Maida Vale. We all hung out in the same bar and the same basement studio, which was in Warrington Crescent. It was a four-track studio owned by our lead guitarist, Matt Dangerfield, and we would do demos there.

Casino lived in Maida Vale in North London, along with a lot of other musicians of the time, including Sid and Gary Holton. Maida Vale was the home of West End prostitutes, and different types of people lived there. A few of the houses were empty, and people used to squat in them. Maida Vale is only a short bus ride from the West End, so it was very convenient as a central and cheap place to live.

Gary Holton was the vocal and front for the London-based band Heavy Metal Kids in the mid and late seventies and then fronted his band, The Gems, and would often bump into The Boys around the gigging circuit in London.

Casino and I hadn't kept in touch after he went back to London after Christmas 1977; of course, I barely knew him at the time, but I was very happy to see him when he moved back to Trondheim in 1980. I heard he had been over for a visit and laid down some tracks with an English friend of his a few months earlier. I caught a glimpse of his mate when he was there, but I had no idea who he was. I just briefly spotted this dark-haired guy with a huge black eye—a really painful-looking shiner—at Nidaros Studios. I think Cas and Gary were in Nidaros Studios for most of the time they were in Norway the first time around.

I heard about it from my friends, as Gary had arrived in Trondheim with his then wife, Donna. Theirs was quite a tempestuous relationship, I was told. I met her briefly in Nidaros Studios one day, when I popped in for some reason. Donna Holton was waiting for Gary to finish singing, and we had a little chat on the brown leather floppy sofa in the waiting room. Nothing exciting, just wondering whether there was any coffee to be had and 'where the hell did they keep the cups' kind of thing. She seemed very nice, and I didn't know what all the fuss was about.

I never thought Casino would move back to Norway, because his band was doing quite well. They had made four albums and were making a name for themselves, being the first punk band to sign for an album deal with a record company (NEMS). The Damned had a single deal with Stiff

Records, and The Sex Pistols had been sacked by EMI at the time.

CASINO STEEL : Yes, but not doing well enough. We were doing all right. We were just about to release our fourth album, but we weren't getting anywhere. I'd just been to Norway and recorded an album with Gary Holton, and I was also playing with The Ramones. They asked me to go to New York with them. They offered our road manager and me a place in their family. At the time, Joey and Johnny Ramone really hated each other, so it wasn't any fun. It was great on stage, but there was no social togetherness at all. I was an alcoholic and a nervous wreck at the time, so I decided I needed to go in a different direction. I turned them down and decided it was also the right time to leave The Boys

I bumped in to Casino Steel one Friday afternoon during the spring of 1980. It was good to see him again, and we stood together in the warm sunshine, chatting for a while and catching up. I hadn't seen him since Christmas 1977, and a lot of water had passed under the bridge in both our lives since then. Sid died the year before in February 1979, before I could see him again after he left Scandinavia. I was still trying to come to terms with his death. It had shocked me, and I wasn't dealing with it very well. It was good to talk, and he asked me to meet him that evening at a disco called Skansen. He was bringing his mate from England with him, and he wanted to introduce me. They had been in the studio and felt the need to relax, go out and have some fun with friends. Skansen was a place we used to frequent a lot, and I knew most of the people there.

My best friend, Marith, and I arrived at the disco at about nine thirty p.m. The club had an age limit of eighteen, and apart from the usual soft drinks, you could only get beer and wine there at the time. Skansen was already filling up when we got there, and the air was heavy with cigarette smoke. This was way back in the day when 'everyone' smoked, and you could cut the air with a knife.

There were a few people dancing to the sound of Funkytown by Lips Inc, blasting out from huge speakers perched on either side of the dance floor. The disc jockey was in his place behind a large desk with a double record player and a microphone. On the floor, there was a battered suitcase, which contained his collection of single records, and another two cardboard boxes beside that, full of vinyl LPs. I watched him check a record closely for scratches before he put it on the player and introduced I'm in the Mood for Dancing, by the Nolans, in a funny voice, mimicking English DJs of the time; being Norwegian, he couldn't really pull it off.

This was before DJs would blend music and scratch records to make a cool transition of sound from one track to the next. We were lucky if he managed to get the right track on the LP he had just introduced in the break between two songs and not get ear-splitting feedback from the speakers. As it was dark, the DJ would use a torch he had on the table beside him to get the record player needle on the right place. It didn't always work well because he had difficulty seeing what he was doing when the disco lights were flashing. It was all a bit hit and miss, really.

Marith and I managed to get a table in the centre of the club, and we sat down. My heart sank when I saw the queue at the bar. It was my turn to get the drinks, so I left Marith alone, eagerly looking around the room to see who was there, and made my way towards the bar and the queue, where I knew I would be stuck for some time.

Casino Steel (front centre) Photo © The Boys

I hadn't seen Cas or his mate, and I knew he probably wouldn't arrive this early. I was getting closer to the barmaid when I suddenly felt someone staring at me. You know how it is when you can feel someone's eyes burn a hole in the back of your head without actually seeing them? I looked around, and there was a dark-haired guy I had never seen before, standing on his own just by our table. He wore jeans he had turned up to three-quarter length and black Doc Martins. He had a red-checked shirt on with the sleeves carelessly rolled up and red braces. His dark hair stood on end at the front but was long at the back, reaching a little over the collar of his shirt in something that resembled a mullet style. There was something very 'British' about him I couldn't quite put my finger on, but I instinctively knew this had to be the friend Casino had told me about.

"Hiya darling, do ya' wanna screw?"

Cheekily, he kept staring and didn't look away, even though he saw I had spotted him. I was getting the barmaid's attention then, and just after I had ordered two beers using sign language, the guy that had been staring at me was suddenly standing beside me in the queue at the bar. He smiled at me, but I ignored him and looked away. The DJ was talking loudly, and I think the barmaid must have been lip-reading, as she couldn't possibly have heard me over the record Boogie Wonderland by Earth, Wind and Fire. While I was paying for the beers, the guy leaned closer to me and said loudly in my ear, "Hiya darling, do ya' wanna screw?" in a broad, cockney accent, followed by a cheeky chuckle. I sensed it was a pick-up line that was meant to shock, more than anything else. Or that he was just trying to be funny. He obviously didn't know I was the person whom I'm guessing Casino had told him he was meeting, and I thought I would have some fun with him. I made a serious face I hoped expressed total disgust or at the very least, indignation. I looked him over from the roots of his hair to the tips of his toes, and I leaned in and said, "I don't screw people like you!" loudly in his ear.

The guy stepped back in surprise and started to laugh. He tried to lean closer to me again to talk to me, but I smiled, picked up my change and two glasses of beer and was just about to make my way back to the table when Casino Steel appeared. Cas is dark with spiky hair and always wears a suit jacket and jeans. He's the only person I know who can make a suit jacket and jeans look punk and über-cool. He had rolled up the jacket sleeves to just below his elbows, which was the trend at the time.

"Hiya, Teddie. I see you've already met Gary, then," he said loudly to us both. He turned to Gary, who was laughing after realising who I was, and it looked as if he was feeling a little bit silly. Gary greeted me with a kiss on each cheek, almost making me spill the beer I was holding and said, "Ahhh, I should have guessed who you were when I heard your English accent. Pleased to meet you, but we can still fuck, yeah?" Cas looked at Gary and shook his head and laughed, as what Gary had said to me was exactly what he expected from him. His outrageous pick-up lines and his attempt at humour weren't outwardly working, but inside I was giggling. I just didn't want him to realise this just yet.

Casino made his way towards the front of the queue at the bar, and people just let him pass; he didn't stand in line for more than thirty seconds. I was well impressed. I turned and made my way back to the table where Marith was sitting and waiting for me, whilst the disc jockey had slowed things down with Suicide is Painless, the theme song for the series M.A.S.H. It had been in the top ten in the charts for weeks, and I personally couldn't stand it. Why anyone would want to listen to that in a disco was beyond me, but the dance floor was crowded with couples dancing together closely. Some looked like they should have got a room, using the darkness and the proximity of their dancing partner to get a crafty squeeze of a buttock or two, and the guys weren't much better either.

"I see you met Cas' friend," Marith said as she put out her cigarette in the ashtray and took a long sip of her beer I'd placed on the table in front of her.

"Yeah." I laughed shaking my head. "What a character."

"I thought it might be him. He doesn't look Norwegian, and he has that London rock-star look about him. He seems overly confident. What's he like?" Marith asked.

The disco was filling up, and it was getting really hot. I took a sip of my beer, too, and looked towards the bar where Casino and Gary were standing, chatting to Casino's blonde sidekick and drummer, Geir Waade. Gary smiled at me sheepishly, and I looked away. The DJ was shouting into the mic, and I couldn't quite catch what he was saying, as half of it was in Norwegian. Then he tried something in broken English, got some feedback sound from the mic, which threatened to deafen people closest to the speakers, and suddenly we were treated to Boney M's Ma Baker. I remember thinking it might be a good idea for the DJ to take himself off to the record shop and update his collection. I yawned and thought to myself that this was going to be a long night.

"He's a bit up his own arse and full of himself," I said to Marith and she laughed.

Casino and Gary made their way towards where we were sitting. Cas stopped to talk to people on the way and introduced Gary to some friends, and then they came to sit with Marith and me. Cas threw his cigarette packet on the table and put his beer glass down, whilst Gary took the chair beside me. He didn't say anything to begin with, leaning back and trying to look disinterested and bored, then he smiled at me and said, "What did you mean by your comment 'people like me'?," Gary asked me after a while, seriously, in a deep cockney accent. I suddenly realised he might have felt hurt by my reply.

"Well, you obviously wanted to shock me with what you said, so I thought I'd be a bit naughty and shock you back," I answered and we both laughed.

"I know the routine—be rude to me to get my attention and then the charm offensive. Sorry, doesn't work with me."

Gary smiled knowingly, nodded approvingly and then made friendly conversation. He asked why I was living in Norway, and I told him a little about my background. He responded by telling me why he was in Norway, and although I was polite, I wasn't really paying attention to begin with. I was glad he had become more at ease. I felt that he used his brand of chat-up lines light-heartedly to get to know people. I was glad I realised that straightaway. He was a really cheeky chap, who oozed coolness, and his charisma was undeniable.

"She looked like Little Bo Peep who'd fallen down a coal chute."

I could see a few of the local girls eyeing him, but he didn't seem to notice, as he was too engrossed in conversation. There were two girls in particular, sitting at the table next to ours, who seemed very interested in what was taking place at our table. They looked a little strange in my opinion. One was wearing a black lace dress that was very short—it could have passed as a top. She had a matching lace headband tied in a large bow on the top of her head. Her hair was messed up and standing on end, as was the fashion in the early eighties. She looked like Little Bo Peep who had fallen down a coal chute. Her friend wore a tight nylon dress that was four sizes too small and almost see-through and clung to her curves like a condom. She was quite voluptuous, and I remember thinking that the chub-rub at the top of her legs, combined with the nylon might get dangerous when she was on the dance floor. The static electricity might have started a fire. Anyway, I'm sure it helped her hair stand on end. It would have saved her a fortune in hairspray. We didn't have the wax and pastes you have today to mould and shape the hair. To get the really messed-up, bed-head look, we sometimes used soap to make our hair stiff and dry and easier to mess up.

"Basically, I'm here to get away from London," Gary said. "If I'd stayed, I would have died. I was getting into all sorts of shit, and it was just depressing. I had to leave my girlfriend, Susan, behind, and that's a pain, but better to spend some time apart rather than find me dead in a ditch one day," he said.

"Perhaps your girlfriend could come and visit you here?" I said, finding it strange that a guy like Gary had a girlfriend. To me, he looked like the archetypical guy who would be seeing lots of girls and spending time with a groupie in the van after the gig, whilst snorting a line or two of cocaine before moving along to the next one and getting drunk with the band. He seemed like a proper 'sex, drugs and rock 'n' roll' type of person, but at the same time, there was something very cheeky and appealing about him. I liked him but made a mental note not to let myself get involved. I intuitively sensed that although Gary Holton was a really likable guy, he would be bad news romantically for any girl. I recognised his larger-than-life personality made him a bit impulsive and rough and ready. He had a need to be noticed, and he liked to be noticed mostly by the ladies. However, as we chatted and I got to know him as a friend, he seemed to relax, and I found him to be both charming and sympathetic. He was fun and interesting to talk to.

Gary kept dropping the names of celebrities he knew in England. Some of the names like Sir Lawrence Olivier, with whom he had acted in the theatre, were of course familiar to me. Others weren't, which I think Gary found a bit odd. I've never been impressed with fame, and I wasn't really into who was who in the music industry. So although I would know who the band Thin Lizzy was, I didn't recognise the name of the singer and front, Phil Lynott, who was a close friend of Gary's. So I just listened and nodded in the right places.

"Cas and I have run away."

Gary took out his wallet and showed me a photograph of a beautiful blonde. I remember thinking she looked a bit like Paula Yates, only prettier. It was his girlfriend, Susan Harrison, who worked as a model in London, and he was obviously very proud of her. I found that endearing.

"I used to be an actor. Acting is where my heart lies. I used to do theatre work, and I spent two years touring with the musical Hair," he said as a way of explaining his background after seeing he had my undivided attention.

"How did you get in to that? Hair, I mean," I asked, seeing I had his full attention—much to the annoyance of the local girl at the next table, who was desperately tossing her hair and shoving her boobs in his direction without much luck.

"Girlfriend, of course. I was so in love I felt physically sick. We had a two-year relationship, and then it ended so I left the show. I only got into singing because the acting roles weren't coming thick and fast. My old man has a pub in the East End of London. I used to help out in the bar. There wasn't anywhere for me to sleep, so when he closed the pub for the night, I'd drag a mattress out and sleep on the floor. That's how down and out I was for a while. Talk about your proverbial starving actor—that was me. I fronted Heavy Metal Kids for a while, and I had my own band, The Gems, after that. We were doing all right, but there are too many temptations in London. It was killing me," he said in his thick cockney accent.

"So Cas and I have run away," Gary added laughing. "Cas has this idea that punkin' up old country-and-western covers is the way to go. I fucking hate country and western. It's shit, but he thinks it's a good idea, so I'm going to be here for a while doing some studio work and just being a lazy sod and enjoying myself and doing all sorts of romantic things like telling local ladies how much I want to fuck them."

"Yes, well, good luck with that," I answered, laughing and nodding towards the young girls at the table beside ours, who were still trying to get his attention. I remember thinking Little Bo Peep would injure herself if she kept tossing her hair and shoving her boobs out at the same time; I'm talking serious whiplash. Gary smiled at me knowingly. It didn't take long before the two girls on the next table had moved over to ours, and I overheard Gary telling Little Bo Peep about his acting career. She listened and looked really impressed. I had to hand it to him: he certainly knew how to chat up the ladies effortlessly.

FAST LIVING

We spent the next few hours together partying and hanging out. People came and went from our table, and although the girls danced to the music at the disco, Gary and Casino didn't. Actually, I never saw either of them on the dance floor that night or later. They only left the table to get more pints at the bar, and they were soon both quite drunk. It didn't matter because so was everyone else.

As it was getting late and the disco was going to close, Casino and Gary, Geir Waade and a few others decided they didn't want to go home and would continue the party at a nightclub called Down Town that was open until three a.m. and served something stronger than beer. I was a lightweight when it came to partying, and Marith and I decided we wanted to go home. I started to get my coat and was looking for a taxi when Gary called to me, as he saw me making my way in the opposite direction to him and Cas.

"Hey, Ted, where are you going?" he asked.

"Home. See you around," I replied as I opened the taxi door.

"No wait!" Gary said as he walked over to where Marith and I were standing. Gary then gave us both a kiss on each cheek. Before walking back to Casino and the others and setting off for the night club, he told us very politely how much he had enjoyed our company and hoped we would be seeing more of each other in future. Marith and I were very impressed with him—such a polite gent in contrast to his rock-and-roll image. Both Marith and I were sure this collaboration between Gary Holton and Casino Steel was something we would be hearing a lot more about, and we turned out to be right.

Chapter 2
Who is Gary Holton?

Gary Holton is probably best known as the actor who played Wayne Winston Norris, the cheeky cockney carpenter in the TV series Auf Wiedersehen, Pet. The series was extremely popular in the UK and around the world when the first series was released in 1983. Auf Wiedersehen, Pet was a comedy/drama about seven British construction workers, who found work in Düsseldorf. It was created by Franc Roddam, and the lead roles were played by Tim Healy, Kevin Whately, Jimmy Nail, Christopher Fairbank, Pat Roach, Tim Spall and, of course, Gary Holton.

Although acting was closest to his heart, Gary was a born entertainer and singer and fronted many bands. With his distinctive coarse cockney voice and larger-than-life stage appearance, Gary was also a musical, charismatic force to be reckoned with.

Gary Frederick Holton was born in Clapham Common in South West London on 22nd September 1952. He was the oldest of three boys: Tony, born 1957 and Nigel in 1961. His parents, Ernie and Joan Holton were pub landlords. They owned The Wellington in Welshpool and the Crown and Sceptre in Minsterley.

Gary attended the Beaufoy Institute children's school and later went to Westminster School for two terms. Having a musical and acting talent and being somewhat of a child acting protégé, he was soon spotted by talent scouts. When he was eleven years old, he got a role in

Quartermass and the Pit. When he was thirteen years old, he acted with Sir Laurence Olivier in *Love for Love* for three seasons. He also appeared in *Much Ado About Nothing*, *Hansel and Gretel* and *Les Enfants*. He had parts at The Old Vic Theatre Company and The Royal Shakespeare Company in Stratford. He also played with the Sadler's Wells Opera Company for three years.

"I love my cheeky chappy dearly."

Gary was fifteen years old when he met June. Her memories, together with those of her friend, Liz, give a unique insight in to the adolescent Gary's life.

JUNE: The brief time knowing Gary was above all memorable, and I love my cheeky chappy dearly.
It was back in 1967 when I first met Gary, an unmistakable star in the making. He was so different to any guy I'd ever met. I had two brothers—one in a band—and there were always guys around playing drums and guitars, so I was used to talent. But Gary had something special. His personality was bigger than him. You knew he was in the room before he knocked on the door.
Ours was a special friendship during our time together. He was my best friend, and I valued our relationship for many years. We met at a singing group at my school, Stockwell Manor, in South London. The group we attended was geared to amateur operatics.
My music teacher suggested a few of us went along for the experience. We both took along our friends—he went with Barry Andrews and Clive Tomlinson, and I with Christine Bentley and Andrea Hutton

Gary and Barry had to walk past my house, so he would always make sure I got home okay and then Andrea, as she lived near Gary and Barry. Gary's need to make sure I got home was a very endearing side to him. Always, no matter what, he would make sure I got home safely. Our friendship continued as just that, while we attended rehearsals and took part in Gilbert and Sullivan's Patience at a small hall in Norbury, South London.

By this time, Gary had been establishing himself in a band. He was born to entertain. He soon joined the same youth club, The White House, at the Oval Kennington. It was here where we—the Lambeth Walk Players—put on another show, which featured wartime songs. We were the artists, the musicians, the directors, the set designers. You name it, we did it. We sold tickets and encouraged our parents to attend.

The one and only night Gary and I laughed so much, I thought we would never get on the stage. Gary and I had to sing two songs together—one was Burlington Bertie and the other was The Lambeth Walk, when the whole cast joined in. All the money we raised went to the youth club, and we just had so much fun.

Following this success, Clive was keen on trying his hand at producing a show, so we went on to perform an excerpt from 'A Man Dies' at St Anselm's Church, Kennington. By this time Gary and I were 'seeing' each other. We were fondly known by our friends as 'Titch and Quackers'. I was only five foot and he was 'crackers'

Gary Holton in top hat. June 3rd from left beside Barry, second from left.

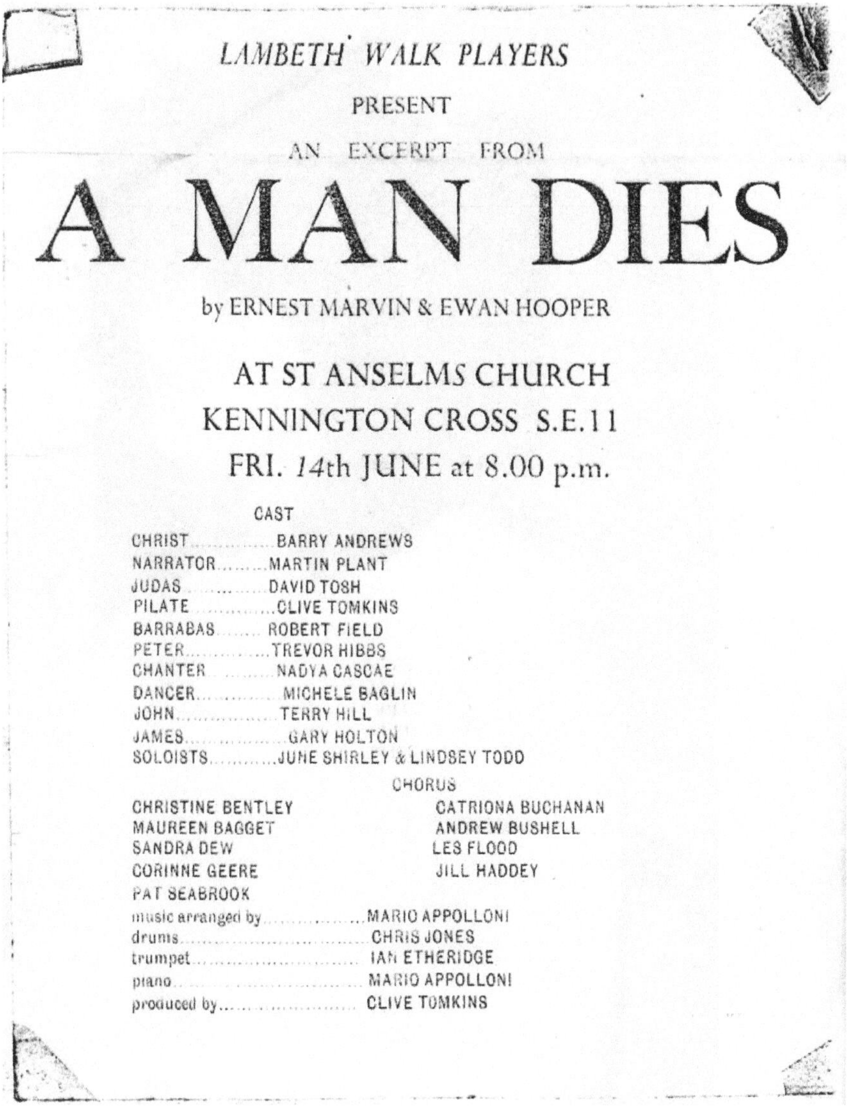

LAMBETH WALK PLAYERS

PRESENT

AN EXCERPT FROM

A MAN DIES

by ERNEST MARVIN & EWAN HOOPER

AT ST ANSELMS CHURCH
KENNINGTON CROSS S.E.11
FRI. 14th JUNE at 8.00 p.m.

CAST

CHRIST	BARRY ANDREWS
NARRATOR	MARTIN PLANT
JUDAS	DAVID TOSH
PILATE	CLIVE TOMKINS
BARRABAS	ROBERT FIELD
PETER	TREVOR HIBBS
CHANTER	NADYA CASCAE
DANCER	MICHELE BAGLIN
JOHN	TERRY HILL
JAMES	GARY HOLTON
SOLOISTS	JUNE SHIRLEY & LINDSEY TODD

CHORUS

CHRISTINE BENTLEY	CATRIONA BUCHANAN
MAUREEN BAGGET	ANDREW BUSHELL
SANDRA DEW	LES FLOOD
CORINNE GEERE	JILL HADDEY
PAT SEABROOK	

music arranged by	MARIO APPOLLONI
drums	CHRIS JONES
trumpet	IAN ETHERIDGE
piano	MARIO APPOLLONI
produced by	CLIVE TOMKINS

Gary Holton Photo © Keith Boyce.

When Gary's parents split up, it was a turbulent time for him, and he went to live with his grandmother, of whom he was very fond. He referred to her as 'me nan'. She loved him to bits and let him use the living room as his bedroom, since there weren't enough bedrooms in the house. He told me he felt 'spoilt rotten'. His parents lived in Ware, and his 'nan' lived in London, near his school. Living with her gave him the opportunity to mould his career.

> **"I thought Gary was highly talented, loved to look good and had a natural charm to make people laugh."**

JUNE: Gary lived with his grandparents in Cleaver Square, Kennington. I would go over there a couple of evenings a week. I would give him a ring, leave my house and catch a bus. By the time I got off the bus at the old blue police box, Gary would be there waiting for me. Whenever possible, on Sunday afternoons, we would catch a bus or a train somewhere. We liked Hampton Court, then we would go back to his nan's for 'tea'. His grandmother made the most amazing poached egg on toast.

Gary's room was an extension of himself. With dark maroon drapes, a wrought-iron bed, a huge mahogany wardrobe and chest of drawers, a record player and posters all around the walls of his idols. And clothes!!!

Gary would play his guitar and sing along to the records. It was during this time that Gary was auditioning for shows like Oliver and Hair. I had a copy of the Hair album, which I took to his house, and we would just play it over and over till he was word-perfect.

I thought Gary was highly talented, loved to look good and had a natural charm to make people laugh.

I would regularly go to the gigs with him and his band. Gary took me to many gigs. One of the most amazing performances we watched was Joe Cocker's gig at the Marquee Club. Then we would all sit and discuss the performances in the Macabre coffee shop next door.

One of the most exciting memories I have of our time together was when he invited me to the 1968 premier of Franco Zeffirelli's Romeo and Juliet in Leicester Square in London. He went with me to Sloane Square to buy a long black crushed-velvet dress. My father took me to Gary's house that night, and he arranged a taxi to take us both to Leicester Square. It was so busy there, the taxi had to stop streets away, and we had to walk the rest of the way. We were so excited, we couldn't talk. Gary looked amazing as only he could, and he made me feel so very special. When he showed the security guards the invitation and they let us in, I couldn't believe I was there. We sat quite a way up and held hands the whole way through, trying to spot all the celebrities.

Gary needed to pursue his career. He had to move on—he wanted to act, to sing and dance, he wanted to be on stage. He wanted to do it all, and that meant he had to attend auditions and rehearsal. It was often difficult to get hold of Gary at this time, as I only had the numbers of phone boxes at stage doors, or I had to call his grandparents and leave messages with them.

We never ended our relationship. We decided it was 'okay', we would stay friends, which we did. We never fell out. After that I only ever saw him on TV.

June introduced Liz to Gary at a party, and she became close to him for a little while.

" ... he had fantastic long hair and smelt of Brut aftershave!"

LIZ : I first met Gary in February 1970 when I was sixteen and he was seventeen. My friend, June, had been out with Gary, and they also did amateur dramatics. Although they had split up, they always remained friends, so she thought we'd be well suited and introduced us to each other at her party at her brother's house in New Addington, near Croydon in Surrey. June and I had lived in the same road in Stockwell, not far from Kennington, and knew each another from infant and junior schools. Although I'd moved to Surrey when I was thirteen, we always remained friends.

I think Gary made quite an impression on me, as my entry in my diary was that he had fantastic long hair and smelt of Brut aftershave! Brut was so popular then, and even we girls wore it as perfume! Two weeks later, much to my surprise, although he hadn't asked for my phone number, Gary phoned me up and asked me if I'd like to go and see his band play at his old school in Kennington London. I said I'd love to, and we arranged to meet outside Kennington Station the following Saturday. I liked Gary and was really looking forward to seeing him again.

I got the tube to Kennington (quite a long journey) and hoped Gary would be there. Luckily he was—a friend had given him a lift in his car. We drove the short distance to Gary's grandparents' house, where he was living at the time. We went into Gary's room, which I assumed would normally have been the living room, and some of the band members and their girlfriends were already there. I felt a little shy, as I didn't know anybody, but they were all really nice, and his lovely nan made coffee for everyone and brought it in on a tray!

The band had a van, and there was a lot of toing and froing to the venue to transport the equipment. I asked Gary what was the name of the band, and he said, "Stonehenge" but pulled a face, so I think perhaps he wasn't too keen on the name! Gary had a bad cold and wanted to find a chemist to buy a cold remedy, hoping it would help him when he had to sing later on.

It was a nice venue—a typical school hall, which was quite large with a stage at one end. The band sound-checked, and then we waited for the audience to arrive. Unfortunately, not many people turned up, but nevertheless, they gave a great performance! I had a really good view, as before the performance began, Gary took me to the side of the stage, found a wooden seat and made me sit on it. I think he was concerned that I didn't know anybody and I would be standing on my own. Whilst he was singing, every now and then he would look over and smile at me, which I thought was very sweet!

After the gig, Gary said he would see me home on the train, but I felt sorry for him, as he had a cold, and it would have been quite a long journey for him there and back, so I said I would phone my dad to see if he would pick me up in the car. We walked to a phone box, realised we had no change, so Gary suggested I make a reverse-charge call, which I did, and my lovely dad agreed to collect me. We walked back to Gary's grandparents' house, and Gary asked me if I'd like anything to eat. I said no, but when he came back with a

really tasty-looking sandwich, I wish I'd said yes. For the next hour, we talked. I think he played his acoustic guitar, and at one point he drew the outline of a snake on a piece of paper and asked me to fill it in with a pattern. I did zigzags and dots. He looked at it and with a serious expression said, "Oh yes, I thought so." I asked him what he meant, but he wouldn't tell me—the more I asked, the more he refused to tell. Of course, I realise now, he was just teasing me, but being so young then, I fell for it hook, line and sinker.

My dad finally arrived, and we said goodbye. Gary said he would give me a ring, and as we drove home, I reflected on how much I'd enjoyed seeing him again, what a great voice he had and hoped he would call me. Well, this is my memory of my date with Gary, a great singer, actor and whom I feel privileged to have known all those years ago.

Although Liz and Gary had a good time, she didn't hear from him after that, but she will always remember him fondly as a really nice guy. At this time, Gary was going to auditions regularly and finally got a role in the musical, Hair, with which he toured for two years. The cast included his best friend, Lionel Morton.

Chapter 3

Heavy Metal Kids Part One

Acting parts in London were difficult to come by, and Gary had been away for over two years, touring with the musical Hair, so when he was asked to front the band Biggles, he eagerly accepted. Bassist and songwriter Ronnie Thomas remembers when he first met Gary.

"I remember he'd go around in fur coats and all that. Very Ken-market look."

RONNIE THOMAS : I was in a band called Heaven, back in 1970, and we were managed by a guy called Rikki Farr, who organised the Isle of White Festival with Bob Dylan. He didn't mess around, but was a really nice guy. He managed a band, Heaven, and we used to rehearse in Ealing in West London—where I come from, actually. In a venue called The Questors Theatre.

Gary was in a band also managed by Rikki, called Biggles. It was Carl Palmer's (Emerson, Lake and Palmer) younger brother. Anyway, Barry Paul, the guitarist whom we eventually ended up with in the final chapter of Heavy Metal Kids, was on the guitar playing a million notes a minute at the time. They had a bass player who was playing all over the place. He was a really good bass player. He actually ended up playing with Gilmore (Pink Floyd) and Morrissey. Lovely guy. I knew all of them. They used to rehearse all Emerson,

Lake and Palmer material, which was way over Gary's head, really. He wasn't into that sort of stuff, and he was just stringing along, cat-wailing over the top of these millions of notes and drum solos. We'd be rehearsing with Heaven, and the drummer with Gary Glitter's band (The Glitter Band), Pete Phipps, was on drums. It was a good line up, and we had Mickey Waller, the original guitarist in Heavy Metal Kids.

It was a nice day, I remember, in the summer, and we all used to go out on the green after rehearsals and just get fucked up in general. Gary would be there because they used to be playing away in the other hall. The doors would be open, and Gary would just sort of stroll out and get stoned with us and just leave them to it. I remember he'd go around in fur coats. Very Kenmarket look. And that's how I got to know him—just getting stoned together, really, between rehearsals. This was around 1970. I think Biggles only did about three or four gigs in all, and then they disbanded.

Drummer and songwriter Keith Boyce, who later worked with Bram Tchaikovsky and Savoy Brown, had been on tour with Long John Baldry and returned to London to take his place with Heaven. They managed to get gigs in France, playing with a French star, Nino Ferrer. They left London and didn't see Gary for a few months. They stayed in Paris for a while before returning to London without their singer in autumn 1972.

KEITH BOYCE : I'd been playing with guitarist Mickey Waller and Ronnie Thomas for about five months in France, and Terry Scott, who was our singer at the time, didn't want to come back to London, as he was having too much of a good time with "des filles à

Paris", so we left him there. On the way back to London, Mickey said he knew a good singer who might be up for joining us. When we hit London, we got Gary down for a blow. I took one look at him, and before he'd sung a note I knew it would work and that he was one of us. Sure enough it sparked from the word go.

Heavy Metal Kids comes from the Burroughs' novel Nova Express .It was actually our management's idea, because we didn't have a name at the time. We'd gone to France and we'd call ourselves the Mickey Finn Blues Band, or just Mickey Finn. When we came back to London we still didn't have a name, and it was our manager who suggested Heavy Metal Kids. At the time it seemed like a good idea. This was before the term 'heavy metal' was in use for heavy metal music. Actually a few years later it started working against us, because we are not heavy metal at all. We are just a hard rock band, so it was a bad choice for a name. Cosmo recently said to me that he thought we should change the name of the band, but I said "It's too late!" It would feel like starting all over again. It's a bit of a double edged sword.

RONNIE THOMAS: We had a singer called Terry Scott, and we all buggered off to the south of France for a while. We were there for about four months in 1972 and ended up in Paris making an album with this really big French star called Nino Ferrer. We stayed at his château. When we went back to England after we'd finished recording with this guy, it was round about November 1972, I think. The singer we had in Heaven (Terry Scott), who was out in France with us, couldn't come back because the police were looking for him. So we were back in England without a singer.

Keith Boyce Photo © Keith Boyce

Gary Holton and Cosmo Tunnel rehearsal 1972 Photo © Keith Boyce

FAST LIVING

RONNIE THOMAS : And Mickey (Waller) says, "Hey, I've got an idea. How about little Gary? I bumped in to him the other night, and Biggles have broken up, and he's looking for something to do." Keith didn't know Gary at that time. Mickey Waller, the guitarist, and I knew him. So we started rehearsing with Gary. That was it, really. Gary was the front-liner all the time. We were almost building the act around him because he was such a personality on stage.

Barry Paul, guitarist and founding member of Biggles, remembers how he met Gary and Heavy Metal Kids.

BARRY PAUL : Going back to the beginning. I founded a band called Biggles. We held auditions for singers. Gary showed up in patched jeans and sat on the floor reading Beano and Dandy comics. He sang and hit some high notes like Terry Reid, so we hired him.
Our manager, Rikki Farr, also had a band which became Heavy Metal Kids, and Gary moved over. At some point I was asked to jam with them, and it worked out pretty well. We set off to St Tropez and Paris with Mickey Waller's connections, and the band got musically tight.

KEITH BOYCE : Nino Ferrer had a load of hits in France in the sixties and into the seventies. We were playing a club called Papagayo in St Tropez. This club used to get a lot of French stars like Brigitte Bardot, Johnny Hallyday, Roger Vadim and people like that. That's where we met Nino. He saw us playing and asked us to be his backing band.

Nino Ferrer, Keith Boyce (standing), Ronnie Thomas Photo © Kinou Ferrer

Heavy Metal Kids formed in autumn 1972. With Gary's hoarse and loud cockney voice, Heavy Metal Kids had a spectacular front man. Gary would put on a show and change costumes several times during every gig. Heavy Metal Kids were going places and Gary became a popular cult figure. For a while, Heavy Metal Kids had two guitarists when Cosmo joined them.

COSMO : **The first time I was briefly introduced to Gary was in 1969/70 in Glasgow in a hairdressing salon, of all places, by a very old friend of mine, Lionel Morton, from the sixties band The Four Pennies. Gary and Lionel were in Glasgow, performing on tour in the musical Hair.**
But it was the next time I saw Gary that was way more memorable and dramatic. It was 1972 in the Speakeasy. I was on stage playing with a band, and Gary came walking down towards the stage shouting at the top of his voice, and we all remember what that's like. "Tell these losers to fuck off. You're joining Heavy Metal Kids!" So I did.
Gary and I were close. I was living with Lionel Morton, who was actually Gary's best friend. We all spent a lot of time together out of Heavy Metal Kids' environment.

KEITH BOYCE : **At the time I met Gary—and this is strange—he was living in the street next to mine. His girlfriend, with whom he was living then, was a girl called Dawn. Lovely hippie sort of girl. Anyway, Gary's girlfriend after Dawn was a French model called Anne Goddet. She, Gary and I and a couple of our roadies rented a house together in Kennington.**

Gary met French model Anne Goddet in 1972, and there was an instant mutual attraction. They both fell deeply in love. Many years later, when Gary was in Norway, we had a silly chat about first loves. In my opinion, Gary was with the love of his life—Susan Harrison—at the time, and he asked me who was my first real true love. It was just a frivolous conversation to fill the tedium at some party or event we both attended. He asked me, "Who was the first guy to knock your socks off, and whom you'll never forget?" It was of course Sid Vicious, and I asked Gary if Susan was that person for him. He thought about it for a few seconds with a smile on his lips and said, "I love Susan so much, it's amazing. She's definitely the one for me, but the first true love I will never forget was a French girl called Anne".

"We went to my place and lived together for four years."

ANNE GODDET : I met Gary one evening at the Speakeasy, a famous night club at the time, where all the new groups used to play. I saw a guy bumping down to the stage, top hat on, very long hair and Wellington boots. I thought he looked amazing. When the group played, I realised he was the singer, and as I knew the guitarist, Mickey Finn (Mickey Waller), he introduced me to him. We had a little chat, but he was with a girl, so I forgot all about him.

A few weeks later, I was again spending the evening at the Speakeasy. I was dancing when someone spoke to me from behind, saying, "I think you're beautiful." It was Gary! I wasn't going to miss it this time, so I answered, "Let's go." He said, "I need a little time to pick up my things." "Okay, but be quick," I answered.

(I was a little drunk, I'm afraid). We went to my place and lived together for four years.

I was working quite successfully as a model in London at the time. I loved watching Gary on stage—he was amazing. I was trying to keep him away from drugs (hard ones, especially coke). I remember one evening he was at the police station (God knows what he said to the cops!), and they were keeping him overnight. He called me to ask me go over and said, "How's Mandy?" We didn't know anybody called Mandy, so I assumed he wanted some Mandrake to put him to sleep, so I took him a marvellous sandwich with powdered Mandrake inside—the worst!

Mandrake is a drug made from a plant from the Belladonna family. It's primarily known for its anaesthetic and supposedly magical properties, but can cause delirium and hallucinations if taken in sufficient quantities. In small quantities it has a similar effect to a painkiller or a sleeping pill.

KEITH BOYCE : The band got on like a house on fire! We had so much fun, and we all had the same slightly surreal sense of humour and our own language. We did have a few disagreements, but we were very close, and we felt like brothers at that time.

FAST LIVING

Postcard from Gary Holton and Anne Goddet when they moved in to their new house in Clapham 1974

FAST LIVING

Anne Goddet on the other side of the card sent out by Gary and Anne when they moved in to their new house 1974

Gary Holton and Anne Goddet

ANNE GODDET : Life was funny with him—joyful and bright. I don't regret a minute of the time we spent together. Though he was only twenty when we first met (I almost collapsed when I found out!), he was a real man, more so than other much older men. He was four years younger than me, and we came from totally different backgrounds, I was taller than him, but we were soulmates. I always have a picture of him in my living room.

COSMO : I knew Anne Goddet very well. She was gorgeous and an absolutely lovely warm and friendly person. I only knew Donna briefly. What can one say about Donna?

RONNIE THOMAS : If we didn't have single rooms on the road and had to double up, he'd always say, "Come on then, Elsie," and we'd share. There was an old musical act called Elsie and Doris Waters. One of them was the sister of Dixon of Dock Green. Anyway, this was back in the fifties or sixties on the radio. They were a couple of comediennes, and they used to camp it up a bit. Anyway, I was Elsie, and the keyboard player that we had was Doris. We had the long hair and the make-up. Nothing queer about it, just a nickname that stuck.

It would always be Gary and I sharing a hotel room, and the first thing we'd do was change everything around. We'd put the wardrobe behind the door so you could barely get in, and all the beds would be flat against the walls and upright. We used to change the whole room around. Not wreck it, just change it around. Then we'd phone up for room service and ask for a couple of drinks to be sent up. And the poor guy would come up and wonder what hotel he was in. Just having fun and kids' stuff really, but you get bored on the road, so you start messing around. We did a lot of weird stuff on the road. There was always something going on.

KEITH BOYCE : I took this photo (next page). It's from 1973 and was taken in London in the garden of the Victoria and Albert Museum, I think. Pete Phipps is a drummer and was originally with Ronnie and Mickey Waller in the band Heaven. He left and joined Gary Glitter, and I took over on drums with Heaven, who then became Heavy Metal Kids. Bob Wills was a singer and our roadie in the early days.

Ronnie Thomas, Gary Holton, Barry Paul, Bob Willis R.I.P. Phil Harris and Pete Phipps Photo © Keith Boyce.

FAST LIVING

From left to right: Pete Phipps, (drummer for the Glitter band and the drummer for Heaven. Keith Boyce replaced Pete in Heaven and they became HMK) Ronnie Thomas, Keith Boyce, Barry Paul, Phil Harris (guitarist and guitar specialist) and Bob Wills (HMK Roadie R.I.P. 1951-2011). Photo taken by Gary Holton
Photo © Keith Boyce

Gary Holton and Keith Boyce Photo © Terry Boazman.

FAST LIVING

Gary Holton Photo © Bernie Reichert

ANNE GODDET : Before I bought a house in Clapham Common, north side, we lived for a while in the house in Kennington with other members of the band, but I don't remember any fire. We were living in a room on the top floor, and we used to act as if we were arguing as soon as we entered the house so that nobody would come and bother us when we wanted to be alone.

KEITH BOYCE : In the summer of 1973, we were back in France with Gary. We went to France to play in St. Tropez for a few weeks at the club the Papagayo. Anyway, after leaving St. Tropez, we went to Paris to do some gigs as Heavy Metal Kids, and at the same time we did a week of live TV sessions with Nino. The program was called Midi Trente. Gary did backing vocals for Nino on this. So we'd get up early each day and rehearse with Nino, then trundle off to this TV station and do a couple of numbers on this show, then we'd shoot off somewhere to do a gig. It was a great time, and Gary loved it.

We lived in a house in Kennington in London, and did we have some fun there! We lived there from 1972 until 1974, when the house burnt down whilst we were on tour. We were on tour in France, and we got back from a gig and got a garbled message from the reception that something had happened to our house in England. So we tried to phone home, but in those days the phones were shocking in France. You either couldn't get a line or get through, and I seem to remember you often had to book a call to be sure to be able to get a line.

> "So this guy turns up and sees the fire and crowd and asks a fireman what was happening, and the fireman replied, "Someone's in the house."

KEITH BOYCE : Anyway, we forgot about it, but when we got home, we drove up to our house only to find there had been a big fire. The roof of the house was gone, and most of Gary and Anne's (Goddet) room with it, as they were on the top floor of this three-storey house. We went into the house, and my room was beneath Gary's on the first floor. My room was wrecked!

The firemen had broken my door down, as it was locked, and everything in the room was covered in soot, soaking wet, and it stank of smoke. All my clothes were wrecked along with photos and records and books, and someone had stolen a load of cash and jewellery to piss me off further. There wasn't much left of Gary's room, as that's where the fire had started.

It transpired that Gary had let a roadie, Rayner, stay in his room while we were away. Rayner was out of it and left an electric fire on when he went over the road to see some girl. Apparently, Rayner was passing out when this girl looked out the window and saw our house on fire. Rayner had left the electric fire on, close to a curtain, and that went up and started the fire.

Luckily, Anne Goddet was away somewhere, but we also had a guy called Robert living there as well. Robert was later Gary's dresser, but at this point he was unemployed, so we just let him live rent-free in the little box room next to Gary's. Robert was lovely but a bit soft—and gay, we thought.

FAST LIVING

On tour in France Pierre, Gary and Ronnie St Tropez, 1973 Photo © Keith Boyce

KEITH BOYCE : Anyway, this girl across the road roused Rayner and called the fire brigade. When the fire brigade turned up, Rayner went to speak with them and told them that Robert was in the house. Of course, there was big panic then, as the fire was raging. Robert's room was at the top, and the firemen were trying to get into the house.

So this guy turns up and sees the fire and crowd and asks a fireman what was happening, and the fireman replied, "Someone's in the house." So this guy says, "Who?" The fireman replied, "A guy called Robert." To which this guy replied, "Robert? But that's me!" And indeed it was, as our Robert had been out, unbeknown to Rayner.

You really had to know Robert and hear the story from him, as he was very camp and funny. I pissed myself laughing when I heard this. Meanwhile, Gary had to move out of the house immediately. Anne had bought a house in Clapham, and Gary moved in there that night, despite it resembling a building site. I think I toughed it out in my room for about a week and tried to clean it up, but I couldn't handle the damp and smell, so I moved in with a girlfriend. Shame, as it was great fun while it lasted in that house.

Danny Augusto Peyronel is a singer, songwriter, keyboard player and producer. Peyronel joined Heavy Metal Kids after being introduced to them by a mutual friend, guitarist Mickey Waller at the Marquee Club in 1973.

Danny Peyronel and Gary Photo © Peyronel

"Gary was ruthless with me to begin with, doing the whole 'breaking in the new boy' thing relentlessly."

DANNY PEYRONEL : I was in my very first ever pro band, The Rats, and we got a gig, opening for Heavy Metal Kids at The Marquee. I can't remember if I even talked to Gary then, but he sure made an impression on me, as did the band, whom I liked instinctively.

In fact, it was that gig which got Mickey, the guitarist, to call me and ask me down to The Tunnel, which was a rehearsal studio we also used. We jammed a bit, and they pretty much asked me to join straightaway. We went on the road a couple of days later, and that was that.

A few months after that, we went into Olympic Studios to record the first album, for Atlantic Records, which was Zeppelin's label, as well as The Stones' at the time.

Gary was ruthless with me to begin with, doing the whole 'breaking in the new boy' thing relentlessly. I remember he used to make fun of my then slightly American accent, in such a cartoony way, which as a really green nineteen-year-old, I found hard to understand. I had been living in New York for about a year, and as a kid I lived in the US for another couple of years...so I guess I must have had something of an accent, though I wasn't aware of it at the time.

And then, suddenly, it was over, this mild form of 'hazing'. I was fully accepted, and Gaz and I shared hotel rooms on a pretty regular basis for the next couple of years.

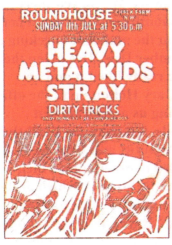 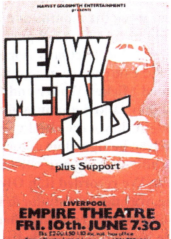

In January 1974, Heavy Metal Kids were discovered by Dave Dee, formerly of Dave Dee, Dozy, Beaky, Mick and Tich, who signed them to Atlantic Records. Dave Dee was Atlantic Records' A&R man at the time, and they were the first signing by Atlantic Records' new London office. They recorded their first self-titled album, which was produced by Dave Dee.

> "Most bands would get ignored at the Speak, but there was no chance of that happening with Gary in the band."

KEITH BOYCE : **Dave first saw us at the Speakeasy which was a very well-known London watering hole for the music business, where we had a sort of residency. This would have been early '73. Most bands would get ignored at the Speak, but there was no chance of that happening with Gary in the band.**
We were a bit rough and ready at that point, but Dave took a chance and gave us a break early on. I can't remember the gig when he saw us. We played there every week for months and months and months. There would always be A&R guys in the audience checking us out, so I don't actually remember Dave Dee being there. He did come to see us and he really liked it and he invited Mickey Waller and Gary Holton up to the office, and they talked him into giving us a deal. He just thought they were cheeky sods, but he really liked the band, so he signed us up to Atlantic, and we were soon in studio making our self-titled debut album, which was great. We recorded it in Olympic Studios, which at the time, was the best studio in London. People like the Rolling Stones recorded there. It was a great studio to be in and we were really happy with that first album.

Danny Peyronel, Gary Holton, Ronnie Thomas and Mickey Waller
Photo © Keith Boyce

FAST LIVING

Ronnie Thomas, Keith Boyce and Gary Holton Photo © Keith Boyce

COSMO : The first time I was fired was by one of our two managers at a gig in London's Rainbow Theatre, for leaning on a pillar on stage and looking at my watch during one of Mickey's extra-long solos. He was considerably less than sober and very out of tune. I was replaced briefly by Danny Peyronel, a poor choice in my opinion, but I remedied this by asking John Sinclair to join Heavy Metal Kids.

After my departure, I was with The Curtis Knight Band, supporting Heavy Metal Kids, a few months later at London's Marquee Club. Ahmet Ertegün, head of Atlantic Records was there. He said, "Which idiot fired him? Get him back in the band or you don't go to the US!" So I was back in Heavy Metal Kids for the second time.

BARRY PAUL : Back in London, I signed the Atlantic contract, and it was that day or the next when complaining about Gary Holton that Ronnie said, "If you feel that way, you should quit."

He was right! I was a guitar rock-star wannabe and blind to the theatrical talent of Gary Holton and the anti-establishment stance of Heavy Metal Kids (later called Punk), so that was that!

I saw them play Biba's Rainbow room once and started to get it. Perhaps it was that ridiculous His Head Fell Off song.

Somehow, I re-joined in 1975. At that point, Gary and I became great friends and spent a lot of time together.

Ronnie Thomas, Gary Holton, Barry Paul and Keith Boyce
Photo © Keith Boyce

FAST LIVING

KEITH BOYCE: My favourite is the first album. We'd had a lot of time to prepare the songs, as we'd been playing them a couple of years before we'd recorded them. I liked the production of that as Dave Dee was quite 'poppy'. It's a clean sound and powerful.

The self-titled album was well received by the press but didn't make much impact with the public. The album led to a TV appearance on the Old Grey Whistle Test and a residency at the London nightclub The Speakeasy. But it was soon time to get back on the road, and 1975 saw Heavy Metal Kids heading for their first US tour. There had been some controversy about the name of the band, which belied the type of music they played, so they decided to call themselves The Kids.

KEITH BOYCE : We only toured with Kiss for two weeks. For some of the dates we were billed as Heavy Metal Kids and some as just The Kids. A big fuck-up from our management and record company. Very Spinal Tap in fact! Because of the name change (I never did find out for sure whether it was the record company's idea or our manager's), our second album, which should have been out at the start of the tour, wasn't released until the end of the tour! So we were there for four months playing to massive crowds with no album to sell! We finally found some copies in a record store in New York the day before we flew back to England! All this delay and fuss over a name change we didn't care about. Stupid or what?

The Kids/Heavy Metal Kids toured the US from February until May 1975, playing support for better-known bands in the US such as Kiss, Alice Cooper and ZZ Top.

They were fired from the Kiss tour for impersonating the band. Kiss had elaborate live performances, which featured fire-breathing, blood-spitting, smoking guitars and shooting rockets. At the time, Kiss wore flamboyant theatrical black-and-white make-up on stage, and nobody knew who they really were. It was a big secret. They would arrive at concerts in scarves to hide their faces. When they had their make-up on, they took on the personas of comic-book-style characters.

> **"Why the hell would we want to impersonate them?"**

COSMO : The US Tour was a total blast from start to finish, I think there was a lot more to being kicked off the Kiss tour than impersonating them.

KEITH BOYCE : In fact, we didn't get kicked off the Kiss tour like that. What happened was we were going down better than Kiss most nights, and they couldn't handle the heat, so they resorted to underhand tricks, like pulling the power on us, sometimes as many as three times a night during our set. So every time that happened, I'd do a drum solo until the power came on again, and despite all this, we'd still go down better than them, as we were better musicians and better performers, and we didn't need all the fireworks and smokescreens that they did!

The rumour about us supposedly impersonating them came about when we arrived at a motel somewhere down south, and there were all these kids around the pool having a party. They saw us pull up and invited us to their party. There was a lot of booze and food and a car parked by the pool with music blaring out, and we were only too pleased to join their party. Only after being there for some time, someone said something, and we twigged that they thought we were Kiss. At this point, it was a bit late to spoil their illusions, so we didn't say anything. How on earth they thought we were Kiss is beyond me, as there were five of us, and we're English!

Anyway, Kiss heard about this and tried to use it as an excuse to get us off the tour. In the end, they had to buy us off the tour. We didn't care, as they weren't cool at all, and we went on tour with Alice Cooper and then ZZ Top and others who were cool.

Kiss are crap now, and they were even worse then. Plus, you can put it in the book that the two main guys were so arrogant and conceited, yet they could barely play their instruments! Ace, the guitarist, and the drummer were sweethearts, but as for the other two...!

A friend of mine was driving Simmons around not so long ago, and he was still going on about us impersonating them. Why the hell would we want to impersonate them? We were doing pretty fine at the time, and I wouldn't have wanted to be seen dead in a band like them! Simmons was overheard still moaning about us all these years later.

About that incident—yeah, we did think it was funny when we realised these kids thought we were Kiss and it was too late to tell them and spoil the fun. I guess they were too drunk and stoned and just wanted to believe we were Kiss.

DANNY PEYRONEL : I was a part of Heavy Metal Kids for just over a couple of years, playing, singing and writing on the first two albums—Heavy Metal Kids and Anvil Chorus—and taking part on the band's only US tour, as well as loads of European and British ones, of course. I still keep my diaries from those days, and we were doing something like three hundred plus gigs a year!

The whole of the US tour was fun. It was my very first tour, and the contrast between our gigs in Britain, especially, and this was vast. The American system was so much more artist-orientated than at home, where you were lucky if you were put in a dressing room that wasn't something slightly better than a toilet, and a crate of Newcastle Brown was your lot.

> "... they caught Gary and me laughing at Simmons from the side of the stage when his hair caught fire...he was trying to put it out by banging his head on the boards."

DANNY PEYRONEL : We were thrilled to be treated so well and with such respect. Everything was different, and the public reacted brilliantly to our show. The very first concert was in this vast indoor stadium with Alice Cooper...it was in the middle of nowhere, and we were sure nobody would show up. Of course, it was packed with ten thousand plus kids, and when the lights went off for us to go on stage, a huge roar erupted, which gave you goosebumps. Alice loved us and especially our Gaz. Alice was just a really kind and encouraging figure. A true star.

Kiss kicked us off the tour because they caught Gary and me laughing at Simmons from the side of the stage, when his hair caught fire doing his so-called 'fire-swallowing' bit and was trying to put it out by banging his head on the boards. How could anyone not have laughed, I ask you?

The difference between these guys and Alice was, quite frankly, an ocean. Alice was a true star with nothing to prove. Quite frankly, we hadn't heard much about Kiss, other than the fire-swallowing thing and that they wore these funny outfits. When they arrived at the first motel we were staying at together, they had scarves around their faces, so nobody could see their real look. Very odd. They weren't particularly friendly, and we didn't seek them out either...in fact, I guess we found the whole thing a bit silly and funny. You have to remember we came from a really Python-esque kind of humour and sarcasm, so this was all a bit much for us.

I don't know anything about sabotaging our opening slot...other than maybe turning the P.A. way down, as most top bands used to do at the time.

"... he would come up and kick me in the bollocks."

RONNIE THOMAS : We'd been touring out there with Alice Cooper. Old Alice, bless him, used to stand stage right every night and watch Gary. He'd be there every night. And you know, Alice Cooper is amazing on stage. His show has spiders and monsters.

Gary was always the centre of attention. That's the way he liked to be. It was the way he lived his life. If you were at a party and Gary walked in, you'd notice him. He had two-hundred-percent charisma.

He and I used to bounce off each other on stage because I used to sing with him, and he would come up and kick me in the bollocks, just messing about.

Gary fell off the stage at one point on the US tour and broke his leg, but that didn't stop him. He played the last few concerts with his leg in plaster. He would hobble out onto the stage on crutches. Nothing could stop him.

RONNIE THOMAS : We had to sack the guitarist, Mickey. He was a lovely guy, but used to do a bit of smack and get really drunk on stage, very much like Keith Richards. He looks like him, too. We had to get rid of Mickey because he was going on stage out of tune. He's a great player, but he was just getting too out of it. It was a really hard thing to do, telling Mickey he was out of the band, but we had to do it. We were on the way up and on the way to make it. We didn't want to go on stage pissed.

KEITH BOYCE : Mickey was very much the driving force in the band in the beginning. He had all the contacts. He had been in a band called the Mickey Finn, from the 60's. They had quite a few minor hits, and he had quite a lot of contacts in the business. Mickey left Heavy Metal Kids and joined Steve Marriotts band before we went on the US tour.

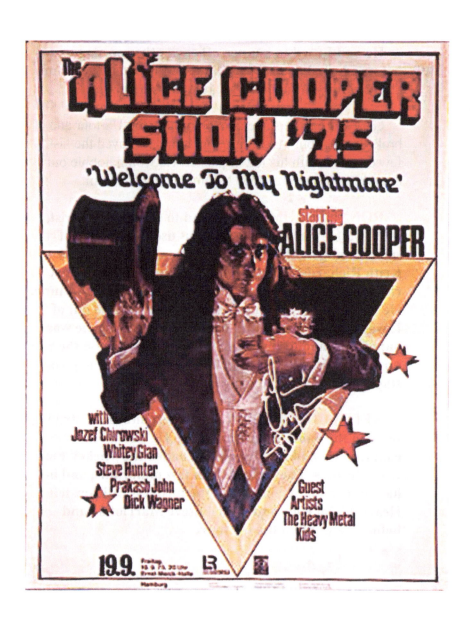

RONNIE THOMAS : We all liked to drink, and we did loads of drugs at the time, like other bands. We always used to do a bit of this and that, but we never got really arseholed on stage, although Keith (Boyce) the drummer, and I did once. We'd done a big New Year's Eve gig at the Marquee Club. You couldn't move in there, and I don't actually remember playing. I can't remember the gig at all. Well, it *was* New Year's Eve, and people kept dropping round to my flat with bottles of this, that and the other. This was early seventies.

KEITH BOYCE : Mickey was such a character and really a very kind-hearted person. Despite his faults, you had to love him. Yeah, he drank too much and did do a little bit of smack and stuff, but he was lovely. Mickey was a very funny guy. In the early days he was very much the driving force in the band, and he had all the connections. For instance, he found Gary, all our early gigs through contacts of his, and he got the band off the ground.

Without Mickey, there would have been no Heavy Metal Kids. He was one of my best friends right up until he died, and I miss him dearly. R.I.P. Mickey Waller 3/3/1947-1/2/2013.

Mickey Waller, R.I.P.

Chapter 4

London Music Scene

What to see and where to be seen

London was the absolute epicentre of the music scene in the mid to late seventies, closely followed by New York. The music scene at the time was in the process of change, and the punk movement was starting to happen. Bands were stripping back their sound to the bare essentials, and long drum solos and complicated guitar riffs were replaced by new, innovative, often politically motivated music. Bands in New York, such as The Velvet Underground, who were managed by Andy Warhol at the time, experimented with their music to the extent that it often bordered on noise.

The financial situation in the UK was bad, and unemployment rates were at an all-time high. Young people in England were angry, out of work and rebellious. Some of them soon realised there were new rules in the way music was being made and appreciated. You no longer had to have expensive drum sets and lessons. You didn't need to play a thousand notes a minute or even be able to read notes. Suddenly, it was accepted that you didn't need more than three chords on the guitar to make a decent tune, and people loved it. They saw it was something they could do themselves, and the punk movement started to grow with the Sex Pistols as the forerunner in London.

American punk-rock photographer Eileen Polk had inside access to the figureheads of the movement. She was Arther 'Killer' Kane's (New York Dolls) girlfriend and later DeeDee Ramone's (The Ramones) girlfriend. She was a close friend of Sid Vicious' mother, Anne, and later close to Sid and Nancy in New York.

EILEEN POLK : **New Yorkers would argue that punk started in New York, not London. I think because the price of a plane ticket was so cheap (about US$250), punk started in both places at the same time. Everyone I knew in New York had been to London. The New York underground scene had been brewing since 1972-73 when the New York Dolls played at the Mercer Arts Centre. But in England, punk really exploded in 1976, and it hit with such power because all the kids in England liked dressing up so much. Punk had a much more visual style in England, but all that crazy hair and living out your fantasy by wearing pipe cleaners in your hair and stuff was very New York, too.**

I remember going out to Ashley's with a dog bone in my hair and a ripped-up animal-print dress like Pebbles Flintstone, in 1974. Most people didn't appreciate it, but my friends did! So people were doing punk-style things before 1975, especially the gay crowd, who liked wearing S&M leather underwear as outerwear.
My girlfriends started the 'lingerie as outerwear' by just hailing a cab and going down to CBGBs in their stripper outfits. I was wearing lace slips to the discos back then because my room-mate, Barbara, had a credit card, and she could justify 'underwear' to her parents as a legitimate expense. So we used to go on 'underwear' shopping sprees and wear the lace slips and teddies as dresses to all the clubs.

It's safe to say that the music scene in London and New York was definitely changing. It was an innovative and exciting time. The punk scene ripped up the rock-and-roll rule book, and suddenly everything was permitted. Eileen with a dog bone in her hair à la Flintstones hair-do sounds more like a yabba-dabba-doo. Gary would change outfits several times during his gigs and wear outrageous Nazi helmets and leather.

KEITH BOYCE : I used to live with Gary during the first couple of years the band was together. There are a thousand and one stories about that place, and what made it even more fun was our front door was about two yards from a really nice pub! Gary really was at his best then, in the early days, and the pair of us would be out and about every night either playing or checking out bands and stuff. I'd love to go back to that scene for a few days. That's probably all I could take now, as the pace would kill me!

Marc 'Frenchy' Gloder, owner of Flicknife Records, was a close friend of Gary's and a major part of the London music scene at the time, having such bands as Hawkwind, The London Cowboys (with Glen Matlock on bass), Alien Sex Fiend, The Barracudas, The Specimen, SOHO, Adamski and Nikki Sudden on his label. The Roebuck was one of the few pubs in London that served punk rockers. They had to go upstairs at the Roebuck to be served, though, and there was always an array of people, such as The Sex Pistols and members of Heavy Metal Kids and others. The Roebuck was the London punk rocker's local boozer.

FRENCHY : I arrived in London in 1975 after spending a year in Crete getting my head together. The first time I met Gary was at the Roebuck pub in 1976.

We got introduced by a punk who knew him. This was a time when punks weren't really accepted into clubs and pubs, as they had a reputation for causing trouble, and the Roebuck was one of the few places that would serve them.

Some of the first people I met when I came back to London were the band that was to become The Sex Pistols. Sid (Vicious) was the first person to call me 'Frenchy'. That's how I got the nickname. The guy who started The Sex Pistols was a guy called Wally Nightingale, when they were called The Strand. He was at school with Paul (Cook) and Steve (Jones).

They were just petty thieves, you know. Wally was a guitar player, and he suggested to the others that instead of stealing junk and getting nicked all the time, why don't we form a band? Wally was the one that really invented The Sex Pistols' sound. Anyway, in the early nineties, I did a single with Wally and Topper Headon. He plugged his guitar in and started playing, and it was just like hearing The Pistols again because he invented the sound.

London's nightlife was dominated by nightclubs with live bands performing. The Speakeasy was a club where you could you could bump into the then rock legends on any given night. It wasn't a very large venue, but because it was frequented by rock stars, international stars and people in the record business, bands would often play for low fees in the hope of being spotted.

The American musician and performer and friend of Gary Holton, Neon Leon, remembers when he first came to London to find fame and fortune and hopefully meet his idols, The Rolling Stones. There was a Swiss heiress who lived in London at the time and was a central figure in the music scene. She is known as Charlotte and lived in The King's Road.

NEON LEON : I was playing in Max's Kansas City (New York), and these gorgeous European women would come in, looking so beautiful, as if they had stepped out of a magazine. Famous people like Catherine Deneuve, Anita Pallenberg, Marianne Faithful and Rose Taylor (Mick Taylor's wife), came and to see us play.

They said to me and Spider (drummer, Pure Hell), "Would you guys like to come to London?" Eileen Polk had been over and taken lots of photos, and it was my dream to go, so I said, "Yeah, definitely!" I packed my things and left with fifty bucks in my pocket. I wound up sitting in The King's Road, and I met Charlotte, who happened to live upstairs. She knew who I was from Rose and the others.

Next thing I knew, I had a room in her flat. I was looking at all the Stones pictures on her wall. They were personal pictures. That evening, Rose Taylor came, and the next day Ronnie Wood and Mick Taylor came over, which freaked me out. The main reason I went to England in the first place was because I wanted to meet The Rolling Stones, and suddenly, there I was in the middle of it.

Mick said I could stay at his place in the country and gave me an amplifier to use and 'Welcome to London'. Ronnie came over to say hi and shake my hand and stuck out a finger. So I took the finger, and he farted and started laughing because he's a clown. He's quite funny. Interesting people would come by. I made friends with Gary Holton and Suzi Quatro. They fixed me up with somewhere to rehearse. We used to hang out at The Speakeasy. I remember it had bordello wallpaper.

Anyway, Eileen (Polk) flew over, bringing the rest of my guitars and all of her cameras, and she photographed everything. This was 1976.

Neon Leon(left) and Eileen Polk (far right) Photo © Eileen Polk

EILEEN POLK : Leon was great about getting me paid jobs! So, after he had been in London a while and was writing back and telling me he was friends with the Rolling Stones and I should come over, I flew to London with his girlfriend, Honey O' Rourke, and several of Leon's guitars in February 1976. Leon knew a lot of people.

We were totally styled by Charlotte and Rose Taylor, who hired a Mercedes and a lovely hotel room at the Blakes Hotel. And we had our hair done at Rikki Burns, where Charlotte modelled, and we had punk hair dye. Mine was dyed black and bright pink.

Then Charlotte invited me to stay with her, Leon, Honey and Spider in a beautiful house (not an apartment) on King's Road. This was at the very beginning of punk, and Malcolm (McLaren) and Vivienne's (Westwood) store was just down the road. I remember going to some party with Leon, and Tori Hamilton (or Dori?) was there with Bad Company. They knew Nancy Spungen, although I never ran into Nancy in London.

There were all these great clubs at that time, like The Speakeasy, Marquee, Tramp (that was private). I still have the brass belt buckle Philip Niarchos bought for me at Tramp (it has 'Tramp of London' on it—a tramp carved in brass). He was a great guy, very charming. That was the night after Charlotte and I had 'modelled' for a hairdresser on King's Road, and I had my first punk hair-colouring.

Charlotte once showed me her photo albums, and there she was with Liz Taylor, Warhol and Roman Polanski on a yacht on the Riviera! She had been a model and actress in the early seventies but had a car accident, which left tiny scars that prevented her from modelling, but she was still very beautiful. When I knew her, she moved in the kind of rich and famous circles that only tolerate discretion. I also met Gary back then, as he was also a close friend of Charlotte's.

FRENCHY : Charlotte's flat wasn't far from mine. It was about two minutes' walk. Charlotte was related to my wife. I actually met Charlotte first. I was going out with this girl called Gina, and one day she said to me she was going to see her cousin, Charlotte, which turned out to be the same place I'd been to earlier.

Charlotte was well liked by people, and her kindness and generosity made her flat a meeting place for those in her close circle of friends. Gary would be a frequent guest and knew most of her friends. This was the underground music scene in London and very little is known about it because discretion was important if you wanted to stay in the company of these people. These were the important people to know, who could help your career should you have needed contacts or money.

EILEEN POLK : I remember Charlotte. I loved her. She was wonderful! She was really nice. I knew she had lots of money—she wore a Lynx coat and had a Gucci phone book with a solid gold pen attached. I'm sure her family was immensely wealthy.
She had done some modelling in the late sixties and was very beautiful too but not that tall. I knew she was friends with The Rolling Stones, and I knew she was subletting the flat on The King's Road from David Bowie (she knew everybody). She was good friends with Rose Taylor, Mick's wife. But she was wonderful and sweet and intelligent—one of the nicest people I met on my first trip to London. Very generous, letting Leon and Spider stay at her home, and all their friends too. She often took us out to dinner. I'm sure Leon got to know a lot of important people because of Charlotte. We used to get into all the best private clubs like Tramp and The Speakeasy. She was a magical, mysterious 1970s' beauty.
We also went to see The Rocky Horror show with the original cast when it was at a theatre in the West End.

That was great! I think The Rocky Horror show had a big influence on the punk scene. The idea was that you could dress anyway you wanted and live out your fantasy life by the way you dressed. There was also a really exclusive club called Morton's in London that Charlotte and her friends belonged to. You couldn't get in without a member signing you in. But I remember Tramp as the most fun club and very fancy with a circular staircase. That's where I met Elton John and Mick Taylor.

NEON LEON : I was in London until late 1976. I went back to New York for a couple of months and then went back to London. When I returned to New York I was suddenly a hero instead of a zero. By that time, everybody knew I'd been living with the Stones in London. It was the big dream for New York bands to go to Europe and play. It changed my whole career.

EILEEN POLK : Charlotte knew a lot of people on the scene and spent some time in New York City. She and her friend (I forget her name but she was Swiss or French), were staying at this huge loft in SoHo that was called 'The Heartbreakers' Loft'. They were a very international crowd. I remember there were big loft beds halfway up the walls and a photo studio with lights and backdrops and a full set of amps and drums to rehearse with.

My Chinese roommate, Anya Phillips, also hung out at the Heartbreakers' Loft a lot. Anya made many trips to London and knew all the bands in London, including Heavy Metal Kids, Gary Glitter, Sparks, etc. Leon was working with a lot of musicians then and used to piss off the 'down and out' crowd at Max's Kansas City by showing up in a Limousine sometimes! I'm sure Charlotte paid for that. As I said, she was very generous. For all I know, her friend was also an heiress.

The New York Dolls had a roadie named Frenchie, who looked just like Johnny Thunders but wasn't French. Whenever Johnny was 'missing in action', Frenchie used to 'stand in' for Johnny in photo sessions.

KEITH BOYCE : We (Gary, our friends and I) used The Speakeasy mainly, and later on we used a cool place you may have heard of, called J. Arthurs on the New King's Road. Some of the staff from The Speak—at least Luigi, as I recall—defected to there. It was cool, as we could all stagger home from there. We sometimes went to Tramp as well, but that was a little too upmarket for us. Pubs we used were the Roebuck (obviously) and The Water Rat around the corner and sometimes The Man in the Moon.

Another late-night drinking hole we all liked was called The Split Coconut, which was up on the Old Brompton Road near the junction of Earl's Court Road. They had these huge cocktails that we'd pass around and share. They were in large brandy glasses, which had a stem but no base, so you couldn't put them down! One would often topple over if someone lost their grip.

Gary's favourite tipple was Special Brew beer, and he liked a gin and tonic from time to time. But the all-time favourite, I would say, was brandy.

I should add that we referred to the three pubs (Roebuck, Water Rat and Man in the Moon) as the Bermuda Triangle, as they did form a triangle, and one would often get lost in that triangle for days.

Chapter 5

Heavy Metal Kids Part two

Heavy Metal Kids went to Island Studios to record their follow-up album, Avril Chorus, which was produced by Andy Johns in 1975. They kept on touring, and it was starting to take its toll on all of them and on Gary in particular. They played over three hundred gigs and travelled on average over a thousand miles a year, and Gary started to hit the bottle. He was drinking a bottle of brandy a day at one point.

KEITH BOYCE : **For the second album we had Andy Johns, who was a great producer and engineer, but unfortunately he'd just come off heroin when we did that album. We didn't know this at the time. So he's off the heroin, but he was drinking like a fish – like 1-2 bottles of Brandy a day in the studio. Consequently I think the album was a bit sloppy, to be honest. It could have been a lot better, and maybe not just his fault, because we hadn't had enough time to prepare for it as we'd been on the road constantly for a year or two. Being constantly on tour, you don't have time to write the songs properly. We were even writing the songs as we were in the studio. It's still a good album though.**

Cosmo and Gary on stage at The Roundhouse, London 1975 Photo © Cosmo

Cosmo and Gary Roundhouse 1975 Photo © Cosmo

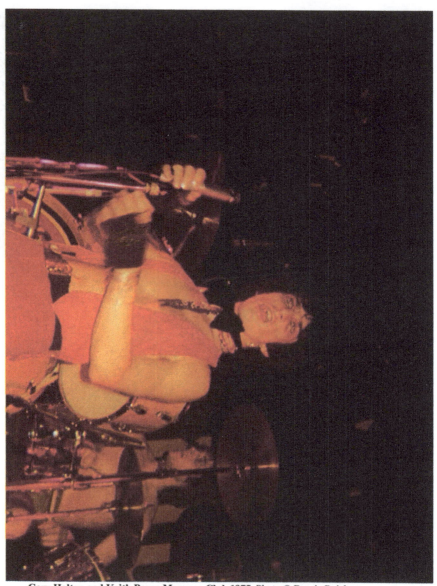

Gary Holton and Keith Boyce Marquee Club 1975 Photo © Bernie Reichert

Cosmo at the Roundhouse London 1975 Photo © Cosmo

FAST LIVING

Mike Quinn, radio host and record producer, remembers his friendship with Gary, which started in 1975, whilst Gary was still in Heavy Metal Kids. Lionel Morton, who introduced Gary to Mike, was ten years older than Gary, and had been his best friend for many years. Morton was the singer in the sixties band, The Four Pennies, who had a number one hit with the song Juliette. He later became a TV presenter for the children's program, Play School, and later, in the seventies, he presented Play Away.

MIKE QUINN : I first met Gary through Lionel Morton. I was living at 127 Mount Street, in Mayfair, which is right in the centre of town. I didn't actually own the flat, I rented it. The guy who owned it was a fella called Frank, and he said to me one day, "I'm bringing the cast of Jesus Christ Superstar around here." The main cast turned up. It was that kind of a flat—a cool groovy, fun place—perfect for parties. They turned up, and Lionel Morton was there, and I said, "Oh, I've met you before. I interviewed you years ago for a magazine." And he remembered, so we had a good rapport straight away. He came in to the studio room, looked at my records and said, "You must have a record here that I could do?" I said, "What are you doing at the moment?" and he said, "I'm playing Jesus in Superstar." Anyway, I did all the jokes—Good God, and all that, but I could see he was quite a serious type of person.
    I suddenly remembered this album I'd bought when I went to a musical. It was called Smike. There was a song in there called Don't Let Life Get You Down, and I thought it was a wonderful song. I played it for him, and he loved it. There were a lot of people at the flat, and he asked them to listen. They all liked it, too. They all

thought it was great, and he said, "I'd like to do that. Would you like to produce it?" I told him that I'd never produced before. Anyway, Lionel had every confidence in me. Lionel is a bit like that. I knew I could do it with a bit of help round me. Lionel was very inspirational. He's that kind of guy. We had to get a lot of money together to hire Mayfair Studios, so we got people to help us. Again Lionel was the instigator. He got me at it, and I got him at it.

Lionel Morton introduced me to Roger Pilkington. He told me he was very well connected, and all his friends were rich. Lionel suggested I show Roger the music business by letting him be my assistant, and all the money we needed would come from Pilkington's friends. That's how we got the money to finance the recording. Roger Pilkington's friends were happy to chip in. There was no shortage of money, as they were all happy with what we were doing. The record we were working on was Don't Let Life Get You Down. Whilst we were doing that, Lionel said, "There's a song I really want to do called Play Away. I've done it before, but I'm not happy with it, and I'd like to do it the right way. I know it can be much better, and we can work together on it." I said "Sure!" So, we worked on Play Away, and that's when Gary Holton came in to my life. Gary came in to the studio, and I was sitting with the engineer, Trevor Vallis. He went on to become quite a big name in the world of production, and this was his first session with us. He was very nervous, because there were about forty people in the studio. At one point he fell off his seat, so I put my arm around him and said, "Look, everything's cool. We'll make this happen, believe me, it will work." Anyway, Trevor was very good.

Gary turned up, and Lionel introduced me to him, and said that perhaps Gary could do one line in the song. So I said, "I don't really know his work. What does he sound like?" We put him in the studio, and he sang in a cockney style. You know Gary had this cockney rhyme thing going on. Anyway, I thought he sounded fantastic. So he sang this line for us, and he was so great, I said to Lionel that we ought to give him a bit more than just one line. So we gave him a verse, which is on the record Play Away. Gary was superb with his cockney accent, and I loved his voice. I thought it was really, really good. Gary was such an outgoing extrovert, that you couldn't help but like him.

RONNIE THOMAS : We were tipped to be really big. We'd done the Reading Festival four years running. We'd broken the box office at The Marquee Club one New Year's Eve. The old Marquee in Wardour Street where everyone used to play—The Stones, The Who. I'd seen them play when I was a kid. Anyway, we did a gig there, and Jack Barry came in afterwards with a big magnum of champagne and said we'd earned it. He said, "You just broke the house record. You got thirty more than Hendrix." Jimi Hendrix had the record at The Marquee. It used to hold a maximum of five hundred people, because of the fire thing, and I think we got well over a thousand in there that night. You couldn't move in the place. We were peaking then, so this would be 1975 or thereabouts.

When Heavy Metal Kids returned from their tour of USA and the album was finished, Danny Peyronel left and went to play with UFO.

DANNY PEYRONEL : Well, Gary and I shared a room most times, and he was directly responsible for my meeting my soulmate, Alexandra, the girl of my life. We're still together, after what's so far been a wonderful life and have an even more wonderful son, Jesse, who's an up-and-coming film and TV director and screenwriter in L.A.

Odd as it may sound, I think Gary and I became closer after I left Heavy Metal Kids and went on to UFO. I guess there was no more band pressure perhaps. I believe we were closer friends. It just wasn't physically possible to be in touch on a very regular basis. I had joined a band that had an almost constant touring schedule, mostly in the US, which kept me away from London for months at a time. After that, I had my own band for a while, and we hung out a bit. We were good mates in that version of Heavy Metal Kids with Barry Paul, Jay Williams and me in the band.

"We both knew there was no way back."

ANNE GODDET : My and Gary's relationship ended in a strange way. He had been violent one evening after we went to see The Who in concert, and I was trying to find a way for him to calm down, especially after he was on stage.

One day I told him, "I'm your mother, your girlfriend, your friend, your sister. It's too much for me, I think we'd better break up." To my surprise he said, "Yes, I think you're right," and that was it! I was so miserable I left England and never returned.

We saw each other again when I was in Paris, a couple of years later, as he was recording an album in the north of Paris. It was as if we never split, but we both knew there was no way back.

KEITH BOYCE: We were tipped to make it big, but we had a lot of bad luck. At one point we got banned from half the venues in England. We did this program on TV called Panorama, and we didn't realize what the program was going to be about. In the end, we found out it was about violence amongst young people, and it painted us in a very bad light. In this one scene there is a part where they are talking about violence amongst young people, and there we are on film doing a gig at the Greyhound pub in London, and Gary was singing the song called *The Cops Are Coming*, and swinging a chain around on stage. Of course this painted us in a really bad light. We felt we were really stitched up when the program aired. As a consequence, all our gigs got cancelled – we couldn't get arrested. All across England, half the venues cancelled the gigs.

We turned up in one town and noticed it was really dead in town. We went into a pub and ordered a drink, and there was just us and the landlord there. We said "It's a bit quiet." And he said "Haven't you heard? Those horrible Heavy Metal Kids are coming to town, so people have shut up shop." This is a couple of years before the Pistols got banned. The Pistols got all their gigs cancelled, but it worked for them as they got tons of publicity about it, but for us it sort of back fired.

In September 1975, Heavy Metal Kids were ready to tour with Alice Cooper again, but this time Alice was coming to Europe. Alice had taken a shine to the band and wanted them as support for his tour.

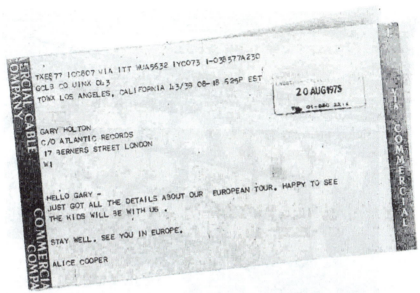

Two good reasons why Alice and everyone else are into kids stuff.

To say that Gary was a magnet to the ladies would be an understatement. They hung around him like flies, and he lapped up the attention.

RONNIE THOMAS : Yeah, he was a ladies' man, and so was I. I had more than he did on the road. Some women were scared of him. Keith and I used to invite the girls to come to the dressing rooms, but they would say they weren't going in if that mad bloke's in there. He was all daggers and Nazi helmets and chains on stage, so they were kinda scared of him. He never took anything seriously. I never did either, and they said we'd never make it because of our attitude, because we didn't give a fuck about anything. We lived in a little bubble. We were working eight days a week at one point. In the Melody Maker magazine we were voted as being the hardest working band with a staggering two hundred and thirty-eight gigs so far that year. We were working really hard and were a very popular act, but it was all a bit tongue in cheek. We didn't take it seriously really, just having loads of laughs.

Gary was living in a house with Phil Lynott (Thin Lizzy). A place over in Neasden, north-west London, I think it was. It was a great big, really strange sort of big house on a housing estate. A number of people came around, including Sid and Nancy. This was about 1977.

KEITH BOYCE : I think Gary might have lived with Phil Lynott a lot later on. It was about this time that they were putting The Greedy Bastards (his band) thing together which was in '78, I think.

Gary Holton and Sid Vicious taken by Phil Lynott © Leona Whitehead

Ronnie Thomas, Barry Paul, Keith Boyce, Gary Holton and John Sinclaire in front of Gary Photo © Keith Boyce

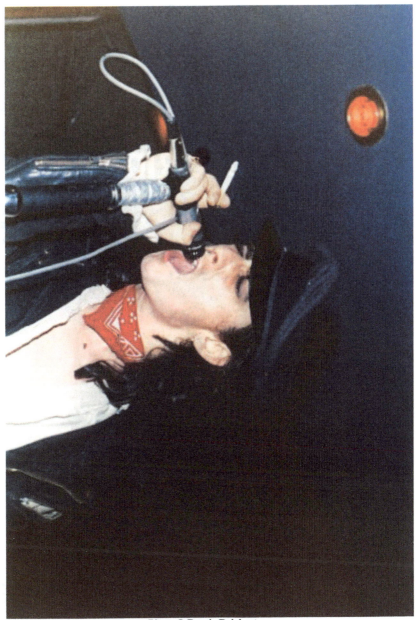

Photo © Bernie Reichert

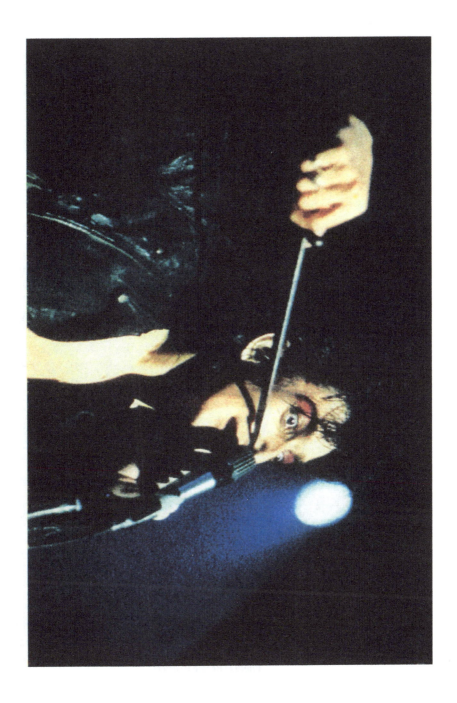

FAST LIVING

Photo © Bernie Reichert

Photo © Bernie Reichert

RONNIE THOMAS : This is when we got a different line-up together. We had an American guy called Jay Williams playing with us, who had been playing with Lou Reed, I thought that was the best line-up really. We did Delirious, but we got caught up in some issues with the record company. We were all getting on at that point. We were all in our late twenties, and there were all these young kids coming up, like Sid Vicious. Sid and Nancy used to use Phil Lynott's house as a shooting gallery. They'd go straight into the bathroom. There was a lot of that going around then—a lot of young kids hanging out there and a lot of drugs on the table, such as smack. It was all a bit heavy.

The band moved to Mickie Most's RAK Records. At the time, Mickie Most was involved with just about everything in the music business. He had played a major part in launching Suzi Quatro's career, to name one.

SUZI QUATRO : Mickie Most and I are both Geminis, so we understood each other. He could be difficult, but then so could I. I give as good as I get—God rest his soul, I miss him. He was my Svengali, and I loved him as a father figure. He made my dreams come true.
    Nobody ever leads me. In fact, I led Mickie. I insisted on leather. He was against it. The 1968 Elvis Comeback Special made my mind up. Although, he did come up with the jumpsuit idea.

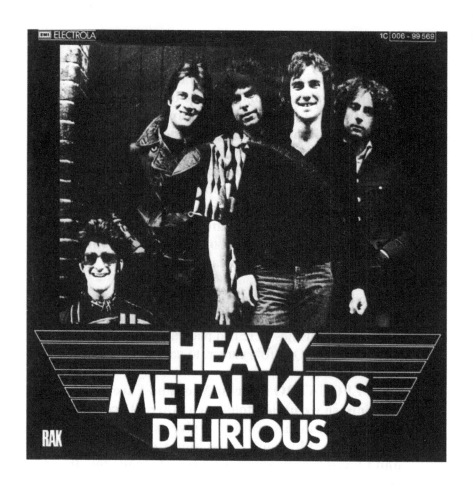

FAST LIVING

Ronnie Thomas, Gary Holton, Barry Paul, Keith Boyce and Jay Williams
Photo © Keith Boyce

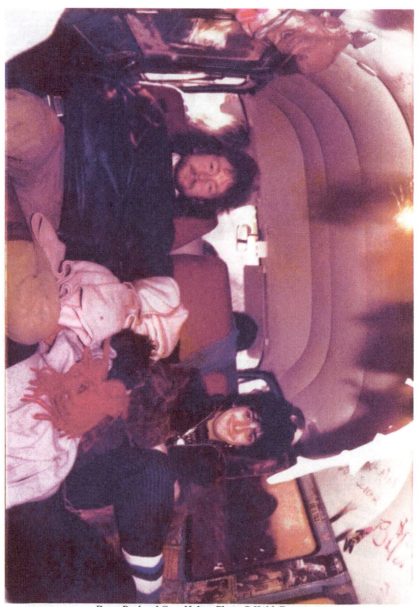

Barry Paul and Gary Holton Photo © Keith Boyce

FAST LIVING

Ronnie Thomas observed there were lots of new kids coming up and making it big in the music industry. Heavy Metal Kids were in their mid-twenties by this time, and the need to make it big soon was becoming ever more important. Last of the Summer Wine* on tour, they were not, but certainly a few years older than some of the young punk rockers who were making a name for themselves.

KEITH BOYCE : We'll we didn't think the up and coming punk bands could play very well. We used to see The Pistols, The Damned and The Clash. All those bands used to come to our gigs before they actually formed bands. These guys were a year or two younger than us. When they did form, we saw them and although we liked the energy, we just didn't think they played very well. We'd been playing since we were 15 years old. We formed Heavy Metal Kids when I was 17 and Gary was 18. By the time the punk thing came along, we'd already been playing for 5-6 years, and we thought we could actually play quite well compared to them. It took me a few months to realize that there was something going on there, and some really good stuff came out of it. We thought the Clash were great, and some of the Pistols stuff was great.

Gary's life was chaotic, and the band was touring extensively. The third album, Kitsch, was released in 1976, and it was obvious Gary was struggling.

---

* UK TV series about old age pensioners in West Yorkshire, England.

KEITH BOYCE: The third album, Kitch, I don't really like at all. The production got all messed up with Mickie Most. We did the backing tracks in France, and then Most took it back to England and went into the studio with it, and he wouldn't let us go in. He was mixing it and he wouldn't let us hear anything. This went on for about 6 or 9 months. There is a lot of orchestration on it.

He got the singers from the band Smokie to do a lot of the harmonies. They were great singers, and it was all very sweet and poppy, which we didn't want. When we finally heard it, we were horrified. I didn't like the drums or the overall production. In the end I felt Mickie Most sucked the energy out of it and it wasn't the Heavy Metal Kids any more. He was remixing it again and again, and I heard you could see through the tapes because all the oxide was coming off it, and it had become an obsession with him. When I tried to tell him I didn't like the way it sounded, he would just ask me "How many hit records have you had?" Obviously he was very successful, and I didn't have any argument to that, because I'd never had a hit record. He'd either say that, or he wouldn't answer and just leave. You'd suddenly see him shooting off on one of his motorbikes or his Porsche. We liked the guy and we got on with him, but it was always 'My way or the Highway', with him. He was a total control freak.

BARRY PAUL: Gary started getting out of it, and the Kitsch album was shelved by Mickie Most. Ronnie and Jay Williams and I kept trying to revive Heavy Metal Kids. I think Keith Boyce was in and out, as he was busy with Bram Tchaikovsky.

KEITH BOYCE : In those days you really had to get on BBC Radio 1. It was the only way you would get a hit. We did the song Delirious, and Mickie Most got his plugger to take it up to the BBC. The single hadn't been released at this point.

There was a panel of people who listened to the records at the BBC, and decided whether they were going to play it. Now the lady who was in charge was about 60 years old—real fuddy-duddy. Anyway she heard the first couple of bars and said, "Eeerr that's a bit weird. Oh no we are not playing that. It's too weird!" So that was it. Mickie thought that since Radio 1 wasn't going to play the song, there was no point in releasing it. We did release in the end, but this was the sort of thing we were up against. We made a few more tracks, which are probably still in the vault at RAK.

Part of us not getting the success we should have had was our fault, because we were irresponsible—taking drugs and drinking too much. We didn't take it seriously enough. Knowing what I know today and if we had taken things more seriously, things would have been very different. Perhaps we could have kept Gary Holton on the straight and narrow in a better way to succeed, but I doubt it would have been possible.

London saw what can only be described as an epidemic of heroin in the late seventies. Some people believe heroin became popular when Jerry Nolan and Johnny Thunders and The Heartbreakers came to London, bringing with them the infamous Nancy Spungen, but heroin had been around long before The Heartbreakers arrived. The band arrived in Britain on 1st December 1976. Heroin suddenly became popular, and people were trying it without knowing how extremely addictive a substance it was or what the long-term effects were. It suddenly became the drug of choice on the music scene.

KEITH BOYCE : No, there was a lot of smack about in London before Johnny (Thunders) got here. In fact, I think it was a friend of mine who introduced Gary to it, around '76. I wish I'd never introduced this friend to Gary, as he was easily lead and probably thought it was glamorous. This friend of mine was pretty hip, so I can see how some people fell for it.

I know dope was a big part of Gary's life, but like you say, the whole London scene was like that then. It was normal to go out for the night and take a couple of Mandies (Mandrakes) and drink like a fish and smoke dope and do whatever else was available then for most musos. It was only a bit later that a lot of people started coming unstuck when heroin crept in.

FRENCHY : Heroin had been rife in England since I first came in 1972. You could buy blues at The Roebuck Pub, but plenty of people there could get you smack in ten minutes.

To say that heroin was a new thing then is completely wrong. In the days of the Raj, loads of people would return from India with huge opium habits, so they would go back there. It's well known that many 'beat' writers of the '50s had heroin habits. So, to say the Dolls or Thunders brought it to England is wrong, one-hundred-percent inaccurate. If anything, Johnny liked London because smack was everywhere and cheap.

After the initial rush of speed-fuelled punk madness, some needed to come down, which is where downers (tuinal, temezepam, valium) and smack came in. But the culture of heroin had been well planted in the UK since the late fifties/early sixties. So not only was it easy to find, but it was cheap too. The thing was that most people I associated with either had old money or were earning well. So they looked upon themselves as drug users rather than junkies. But it comes to a point where you have to make a choice: stop or die.

RONNIE THOMAS : Well, Gary had a drug problem. That's well documented. We'd just got an album out with Mickie Most, and we were doing Top of the Pops. Things were going really well, and then Gary started dabbling with scag (heroin). It was getting a bit too hard to handle. I mean, we'd come so far. We were going out for a couple of thousand pounds a night. In the seventies, that was a lot of money. We were flying here, there and everywhere. Mickie Most was a big shot in the business. He was managing all the big bands.

KEITH BOYCE : One thing definitely killed it for us: She's No Angel, is a great song, and we went on Top of the Pops. I was sure that this performance would crack it open for Heavy Metal Kids. Everyone used to mime on Top of The Pops, but the week we went on they wanted to do an experiment and make one band play live—of course that was us.

First they set all the mikes up and all the guitar amps up on the stage. Then the producer of the show said we couldn't have them there, and made us put the amps underneath the stage. Then they said we were playing too loud, and we had to turn them down. Then they took all the mikes off the drum kit, and left me with only one mike. We had Mickie Most with us and he was in the control room, but they wouldn't let him touch the controls, and he was going mad.

We ended up sounding really puny compared to what the record really sounded like, because we had to play live. That killed it for us, I think. The record was selling about 1000 copies a day, and after we did Top of the Pops, it just dropped out of the charts. I watched it on TV the next day and I felt really stitched up. That really put the nail in the coffin.

"I used to do a lot of drugs myself, but I never got into scag. That was a NO-NO!"

RONNIE THOMAS : What happened was that the band split up. We were going to sack Gary because we couldn't work with him anymore. His whole personality changed. We were a band of brothers, you've got to remember this. I was the best man at his wedding. On the road we were all best mates.

I mean, I used to do a lot of drugs myself, but I never got into scag. That was a NO-NO! But it was a sort of choice drug around about that time, mid-seventies. Steve Marriott was sort of dabbling. I mean, Steve was on the uptown bus. I mean, even he started. Phil Lynott obviously, that was common knowledge. I never saw Gary fix up. He was always saying, "Come on, Ron. Come up to the room. If you don't like needles, I'll fix you up"

EILEEN POLK : I remember the pre-punk scene when people were just starting to buy Malcolm (McLaren) and Vivienne's (Westwood) clothes, and The Sex Pistols were just a rumour. The scene was so beautiful. Everybody was friends, rich and poor, black, white, gay or straight, Chinese, French, Swiss, and everybody was smoking hashish—not doing heroin. It was a magical time, and it only lasted a few short years before being ruined with hard drugs and violence, which was caused by the media telling everyone about 'drugs and violence'. That brought the predators into what was previously a very cool scene.

I also remember being shocked that the cool London scene I experienced in 1976 had been totally inundated with hard drugs by the time I went back in 1978 and 1979. So I wouldn't take a story about drugs as an unusual one. Everyone was a junkie in London in 1979. It was even worse than New York, which got really bad after 1979 when the Mudd Club opened in TriBeCa, and all those clubs in the lower east side, like The Nursery (a club that Sid liked to go to and I hated).

Heavy Metal Kids were dropped by their label, RAK, due to an embarrassing set of events that humiliated Mickie Most into cutting them off completely.

KEITH BOYCE : It was all due to a big mix up one night, that we got fired. We were doing a gig at the Marquee, and we had punk guy, a friend of ours, called 'Pete the Murderer' on the door. I'm not sure if he ever actually murdered anyone, but he was a really heavy punk. We had a small guest list and we told Pete the Murderer not to let anyone in for free who's not on the guest list. Everyone has got to pay. So we left him on the door with the guest list and a couple of other guys.

Suddenly, Mickie Most just turned up. He'd bought executives of the Japanese record company EMI over to London. So Most turns up with all these Japanese people, and tells the guy at the door who he is, and wants to be let in. Pete the Murderer says, "I don't care who you are. You are not on the list and therefore you are not getting in for free!" Of course Mickie was really embarrassed, so he stormed off.

The next day we realized what had happened, and we phoned his office and his secretary wouldn't let us speak to him—and that was it—end of deal. He blew us out! We weren't that bothered at the time, because we never took things seriously. We were all laughing about it.

Max Splodge is the singer and songwriter in the English punk-rock band Splodgenessabounds. They had a big hit with Two Pints of Lager and a Packet of Crisps in 1980. The title inspired the BBC for a TV sitcom. The hit was followed by several albums, and later Max featured in the film Rock School with Gene Simmons (Kiss). Max was a close friend of Gary's.

MAX SPLODGE : I met Gary back in…I think it was 1976. I met him in a pub called The Ship, in Wardour Street. We got talking, and he dragged me off to a night club everyone used to go to, called The Speakeasy. We just ended up with this drinking session that went on for about three days. And then we were mates forever after that. We would be hanging out together whenever he was in town or I was in town. He used to come to my gigs, and I used to go to his.

Ronnie Thomas, Gary's dresser, and Gary Holton Photo © Keith Boyce

FAST LIVING

Ronnie Thomas, Gary Holton, Barry Paul, John Sinclaire and Keith Boyce. Taken at Barbarellas 1976 Photo © Keith Boyce

ALAN BUTCHER : I was a music journalist writing for Zigzag, New York Rocker and others, including my own fanzine called LiveWiRe. My dad was best friends with Keith Boyce's dad at school. Keith was the drummer with Heavy Metal Kids. I did know Gary. He came along to a few The Boys gigs and was friends with Johnny Altman, who replaced him as singer with Heavy Metal Kids for a while. I remember a couple of incidents. We were in Hastings, where he asked me to go upstairs to help get the gig ready. Whilst there, Gary nicked a lot of booze and hid it behind the curtains, so we never had to pay for any later.

By 1977, Gary was dating pretty wealthy socialite Tracey Boyle. Tracey came from a privileged background and was used to getting everything that money could buy. Gary and Tracey fell in love, something her parents fiercely disapproved of. They lived in squalor and moved from bedsit to bedsit, leaving a trail of unpaid bills for Tracey's wealthy father to pick up. Tracey had an allowance, which her father cut off as a way of trying to get her to see that she had to leave her punk-rock lover and return home to her family.

Gary later told me that Tracey had asthma and needed medication but decided that since her parents had cut off her money, she wouldn't take her medication, as she couldn't afford to buy it. Gary told me he thought it was probably her way of trying to punish her parents for not supporting her in her choice of boyfriend.

BARRY PAUL : I used to see Gary all the time then—'77-'79—at the Roebuck in Chelsea. And we did gigs here and there.

I knew Tracey Boyle quite well. A girlfriend of mine said, "I liked her. She was gorgeous but not really aware of it like a lot of them." Which sums her up well.

During December 1977, Tracey and Gary had been arguing more than usual. Theirs was a tempestuous relationship. They were living in yet another bedsit and joined by friends for what can only be described as a heavy drinking party. Gary was very drunk when Tracey collapsed on the sofa and choked to death on her own vomit. Gary told me years later that he was too drunk to help and too shocked and scared to move. The other friends at the party tried to revive Tracey and called an ambulance. Tracey was taken to the hospital and was later pronounced dead.

KEITH BOYCE : I knew Tracey well. She was a lovely girl. Unfortunately, I think she bought into this 'live fast, die young' thing that Gary was into. She, along with some others in our crowd, died way too young. I'm afraid they all seemed to think they were invincible back then.

Tracey Boyle was born into a wealthy family and had everything to live for. Yet, here she was, drinking herself into alcoholic oblivion with her punk-rock boyfriend. She died in poverty, aged only nineteen.

Gary later told me that Tracey's death affected him deeply, and he struggled to come to terms with it. He felt guilty for not being able to help Tracey, but he didn't feel responsible for her death. He was deeply saddened by it. He told me that he was threatened after Tracey's death. He said certain people believed he was responsible and blamed him. The threats were very real and frightened him. He did reveal to me who made the threats, but swore me to secrecy. Gary decided he would leave London for a little while until things calmed down. He would take some time out to grieve.

> "I got the impression he was just heartbroken and grieving."

FRENCHY : I met Tracey Boyle a few times although I didn't know her well. I wasn't in the flat when she died. She was an asthmatic. I remember Gary ringing me and telling me Tracey had died, and he was going off for a while, but he never said anything about getting threatened. I got the impression he was just heartbroken and grieving. I just thought he wanted time to himself. I never imagined he had been threatened. He could have been, of course. It's possible. I don't know who would have threatened him, really. I can't understand why anyone would blame Gary for Tracey's death. She was just like everyone else and didn't need help to getting into trouble.

KEITH BOYCE: I think it was actually late 1976 or even early 1977 when we fired Gary. He was becoming very hard to work with due to his state of mind. Sure, he was taking drugs, but with hindsight, there may have been too much pressure on him, as we worked more than three hundred days of the year. Even on days off Gary would have to do interviews and stuff, so he was never off duty, so to speak, and it was hard going.

Gary was a really great guy, but when he was on the drugs he got really nasty. We got dropped by RAK and there was this other record company who was interested in us. This guy was going to sign us up to Private Stock Records which was Blondie's label at the time. So what does Gary do? Well we got this gig at the time at a place called The Music Machine in London. It had quite a high stage – about 7 feet off the ground.

The manager, who was going to sign us to Private Stock Records, turns up and he's really keen, so we'd got the record deal, more or less. The guy is standing at the side of the stage. So we come on stage, and Gary comes on—smacked out of his head. He goes up to the front of the stage, and Gary goes straight over the monitor and into the audience—almost knocking himself out. I looked at this manager and he looked at me and he just shook his head. He walked out the side door and that was the last we saw of him. That was it for the record deal, and that was it with the band for me. I couldn't work with Gary any more, he was too unreliable.

Well, after we sacked Gary, we spent months auditioning singers, something like three to four hundred in fact! There were a few good ones, but in the end, we didn't know if we were coming or going, so we couldn't decide who was good and who wasn't. The real problem was Gary was such a character that no-one stood a chance, unless a Mick Jagger or Alice Cooper had walked in the door!

In the end, after about four or five months of this, we asked Gary to come back, which he did. This worked out pretty well at first, as he was on his best behaviour, but by late 1978, he was taking more drugs than ever. I ended up leaving the band, as I couldn't take it anymore. He was so unpredictable. The band then carried on for some months with a few other drummers, but then split for good after Gary had a heart attack in Germany from overdoing it.

"Gary died last night in hospital."

RONNIE THOMAS : We actually did get back together with this American guitarist. We went out and made another record with Mickie Most again, and Gary was all right, but he still had a drug problem and just misbehaved on stage one night. It was somewhere like the Isle of Man.

We got about two thousand quid, and Pierre, our percy, (personal road manager) had all the money in a brief case. At about midnight, Gary and Jay, the American guitarist, went in to Pierre's room while Pierre was asleep and got the money out of the brief case, went down this casino and blew the lot on the black-jack tables. He would do stuff like that.

Gary was misbehaving more often, and the other band members were getting more and more frustrated with him. The straw that broke the camel's back happened in Germany in late 1978.

RONNIE THOMAS: On another night in Germany, it got especially bad. We were on this big tour of Germany when we got back together, after the first time he left. I remember I was in the van—I was going off with some girl. I was going in to some restaurant because I was meeting a girlfriend of mine. This German girl was an ex of Keith Richards, strangely enough.

But anyway, I was in the van, and they were just going to drop me off. Gary was in the back of the van with this really suspicious-looking girl. She was a German junkie, and he was rummaging around in her handbag. He says, "Watcha got in here then, love?" and he pulled out a little bottle. "What's this?" he asked. "Methadone," she replied, and he drank the lot.

So they drop me off at the gaff, and they left. At ten o'clock the next morning, I went back to the hotel, The Ramada. I'd said goodbye to my girl in Munich. Anyway, I got to the hotel, and I was waiting for the lift to get into the room where I'd left my suitcase.

Anyway, the lift door opened, and Jay, the American guy, walked out. I said, "Hello, Jay. What time we leaving for the next gig?" and he replied, "Gig's off, and Gary died last night!" I said, "WHAT?" and he repeated, "Gary died last night in hospital, but they brought him back to life again! They should have let the mother die!" He was really pissed off. Gary was in hospital for three days, so we lost three days' worth of gigs. He overdosed, and it wasn't the first time.

KEITH BOYCE : Yeah, it's complicated. About Gary dying in Germany—that was the last tour the band did. They begged me to go, but I'd had enough by then. They took some young kid on drums from a band called, funnily enough, Dead End Kids.

The drummer with Dead End Kids, Ricky Squires, was asked to take Keith's place for the tour of Germany.

RICKY SQUIRES : I was really only just getting to know the guys when we left for Germany. Apart from seeing them at gigs, I only met them a couple of times in a pub in Chelsea, prior to being asked to do the tour. Thrown in at the deep end, I had to learn all the songs on the Kitch album, ready for the one audition-cum-rehearsal I would get before the tour. At this time, I wasn't really aware of Keith's reasons for leaving, except that there had been some issues with Gary, and he'd had enough.
There was an air of apprehension at the rehearsal, I suppose, since the guys were obviously disappointed that Keith was missing, although they didn't in any way make me feel uncomfortable or unwelcome. Gary was also late, and it became apparent they couldn't be sure he would turn up. I was just glad to have the opportunity to play with The Kids, so was wholly focused on being up to the task. We rehearsed some tracks in Gary's absence, but then he breezed in, seemingly happy and unfazed, oozing confidence. He grabbed the mic, and the performer took over.

Thankfully, they were all happy that I'd done enough work and felt confident enough that I could pull it off. So, off to Germany we went.

I remember we all joined the tour minibus and went to collect Gary for the trip. He emerged from his house wearing a large and loud Hawaiian shirt, huge colourful plastic sunglasses and that cocky big grin of his. He addressed us all with, "Wat? Dressed for goin' abroad, ain' I," in his best cockney accent. He certainly got everyone's attention. I was soon to realise this was typical of the big animated character Gary could be. I personally felt really comfortable with him, and I felt that he, like the others, made every effort to help me settle in. Gary and I happened to be chatting at one point later, and he told me not to worry if I noticed a bit of an atmosphere, assuring me that it wouldn't be anything to do with me being there. The subject was quickly changed, and so I thought it best to leave it there.

The sound-check at the first gig was done, and the usual pre-gig adrenaline build-up ensued. I probably and understandably had a lot more pre-gig nerves than the others, under the circumstances, but they had an infectious air of confidence about them that helped me feel up and ready for it. In the off-stage room, where we waited before going on, Gary, with beer in hand, seemed to be constantly but harmlessly joking around and standing up on a table, etc. On stage, the atmosphere was electric for me. With the onslaught of rocking guitars, thunderous bass and Gary in full control of the out-front proceedings, I had an absolute blast.

It was the next day when I was told by the sound engineer, with whom I shared a hotel room, that the next gig would probably be cancelled because Gary was in hospital. He went on to explain that Gary had died in the ambulance en route to the hospital, but the medics had thankfully managed to bring him back to life. He would, however, be staying in hospital to recover. Apparently, having already OD'd on drugs and alcohol that night wasn't enough for Gary, so he proceeded to consume everything in the minibar in his room as well. As I understood it, he was found there, and an ambulance had to be called. I wasn't witness to any of this but was just hoping Gary would be okay.

"When the ambulance guys got there they pronounced Gary dead."

RICKY SQUIRES : Anyway, he continued to tell me this was quite typical of the kind of behaviour from Gary the others had become used to tolerating over the years. If it wasn't hospital, it was likely to be a police station. The other guys liked to party, too, but Gary seemed to have to take it all too far. When Gary did reappear, he was larger than life with no obvious signs of injury or regret. Laughing and joking, business as usual. Now I had an insight into why the future of the band was extremely uncertain and why the other guys were so pissed off. No wonder! This bunch of really talented guys had all obviously worked really hard to create this 'up with the best' rock band, who, in my view, should have become one of the biggest bands on the world stage. They were clearly frustrated and disappointed to watch a successful future fading away in favour of livin' life at a hundred miles an hour.

KEITH BOYCE : Anyway, they had only been in Germany a few days, and as I think you know, Barry woke up and saw Gary was blue and called an ambulance. When the ambulance guys got there, they pronounced Gary dead but managed to revive him. Gary was in hospital for days, and the tour was cancelled. The boys came back stone broke to London and were all well pissed off with Gary. I then did one last gig with them at The Music Machine in Camden, and that was the end of the band.

RICKY SQUIRES : On the ferry journey back to the UK, there was, I felt, a strong air of dejection amongst the guys. I thought they were all just tired and reflecting on recent events. In my head, I was looking forward to all this being forgotten about and hoping I would get the opportunity to have a long future with Heavy Metal Kids. This ideal was soon shattered when I was told the reason for the long faces was that they had made the decision to split. I thought this was an absolute disaster, and I, possibly naively, spent much of the journey trying to convince Ronnie that they should reconsider what they were doing. My efforts failed, anyway, as the guys' determination to split was too strong. Ronnie said he appreciated where I was coming from, but it was too late. They had already tried everything in the past and had just been putting up with it for too long. There was no way he could see it being any different in the future. I thought Gary was a smashin' guy, but his free-spirit attitude and energy couldn't be tamed or contained. I was totally gutted as well by this time, as it became obvious there was no way back.

I will always remember Gary from the first time I went to see the band at the Marquee on Wardour Street. Heavy Metal Kids was one of the most powerful and engaging bands I had ever seen. Gary's performance and ability to command the audience was pretty unique. I will mostly remember my encounters with him during my relatively short time in the band. I'm sure Keith would agree that sharing the stage with Gary, Ronnie, Baz and Jay was an experience any drummer could be proud of.

During the years Heavy Metal Kids played together, the line-up changed several times. I find it confusing and therefore haven't even attempted to write about it. Keith Boyce will explain it to you.

KEITH BOYCE : The band history is complicated. Gary, Ronnie and I were always in the band, but we had four guitarists and three keyboard players. To make it more complicated, two of the guitarists—that's Cosmo and Barry—were in the band twice. Both left the first time around and came back later.
Anyway, in the beginning (this is 1972), it was me, Ronnie, Mickey and a keyboard player, Brian Johnston. We had just come back from France and needed a singer, and we found Gary. We started gigging, and Brian left, so we got Cosmo in, and we then had two guitarists. Cosmo left after some time, and we then got Barry Paul in. Barry Paul left the day we signed to Atlantic records, as he reckoned Gary couldn't sing! So we then got Danny Peyronel in on keyboards. Just before we did our second album, Mickey Waller left the band and joined Steve Marriott's Allstars. So Cosmo came back in the band, and we went to the States with this line-up in February 1975.
When we came back from the States after nearly four months, we fired Danny Peyronel. He joined UFO. So we got John Sinclair in the band on keyboards. Then

Cosmo left the band again, and we got Barry Paul back in on guitar! We did our third album, Kitsch, with Barry and John, and then we ended up firing Gary, as his drug-taking was out of control.

We spent three months auditioning singers. I think we tried over two hundred. None of them right for the band. In the end, John Sinclair left, and I found this American guitarist, Jay Williams, to take his place. We then got Gary back in the band, as he had cleaned up his act somewhat. This was the final line-up, and I stayed until Gary went off the rails again, but I couldn't handle it. The band then had a couple of drummers for the last few months, until it finally all fell apart in late '78.

Right, did you get that? Keith lost me after 'four guitarists and three keyboard players'. Anyway, this time it was over for good. The other members of Heavy Metal Kids had had enough. After the drummer, Keith Boyce, left, they eventually split up.

Chapter 6
What Gary Did Next

After Gary was loudly fired by Heavy Metal Kids for dying in Germany and being a pain in the backside in general, he started to get back into acting, taking on small television roles and TV commercials. He was keen to keep his music career going and was looking for a new band during 1978.

Gary had briefly been on a tour of Scotland with The Damned, replacing David Vanian, who had done one of his disappearing acts. It was to be a short guest performance, as Gary forgot all the lyrics at the first gig and ended up repeating one word over and over: neat, neat, neat. Of course, it didn't take long until the guests were deeply unimpressed and the bottles started flying.

Gary met Pretty Boy Floyd and the Gems, whose singer had just left, and he joined them. The line-up was Martin Hughs (drums), Mark Robbins (keyboard/sax/guitar), Dennis Forbes (lead guitar), Don McNielly (bass) and Gary Holton (lead vocal). The Gems went into the studio to record their album, *Shooting the Singer is No Way to Stop the Opera*, supervised by Chris Tsangarides, and followed by a nationwide tour in 1978-1979.

Before the tour, they were playing warm-up gigs at The Nashville in Kensington, Rock Garden in Covent Garden and Dingwalls in Camden, to name a few.

Gary and the Gems Photo © Terry Boazmon

Gary and the Gems Photo © Terry Boazmon

FAST LIVING

GLEN MATLOCK (Sex Pistols) : I first met Gary in The Roebuck. I remember seeing Heavy Metal Kids a few times. They used to play at The Greyhound. They played where The Rocky Horror Show was on The King's Road. I quite liked Heavy Metal Kids. They sounded quite good and had a lot going for them, despite not having any top tunes. He was a bit of a boy, Gary. He lived near me. We didn't know each other that well to begin with, although we were aware of each other.

I remember once getting on a bus, and he was on the top deck with his mate. It was about eleven o' clock in the morning. Anyway, Gary said to his mate, "Right, I'd better get off here. Anyway, that was a great night out." Eleven o'clock in the morning!

Gary met his wife, Donna, in a night club in 1979. They had a whirlwind relationship, and married a few months later. In an interview with News of the World in 1985, after Gary's death, Donna says she spent months helping Gary get off the drugs. She also says that she knew Gary was seeing other girls, but it didn't bother her and that Gary didn't know what he wanted: a family or fame and fortune. Gary told me many years later that his relationship with Donna was a special one. He said he could always rely on her. His exact words were, "If I get really unstuck and in deep shit, I'll go and see my wife, Donna. She always says no to begin with, but I know I can get her to soften up and help me." I registered the warmth in his voice when he spoke of her, even though their relationship hadn't lasted.

MAX SPLODGE : Donna and Gary would fight all the time. They got married within a very short space of time after getting together. I met Donna and Gary when

they came to one of my shows at the Victoria, and she was playing up. I said to my mates in my band that it wasn't going to last ten minutes. Bloody chaos. World War Three when they were about. Gary tried to get in touch with me. I was away playing when he had the wedding at Marylebone registry office. Obviously, I couldn't get there. And by the time I came back from my tour, they weren't together any more.

"He looked like the archetypal rock 'n' roll front man, and he also drank like one."

Gary's acting career started to take off in 1979, and he played the character Eddie Hairstyle in the television movie The Knowledge, with Michael Elphick and Kim Taylforth. He starred with Toyah Wilcox as Mole in the television series Shoestring and then played the lead role, as Ken, in Stephen Frear's 1979 film, Bloody Kids. He also had an unaccredited role in The Who film, Quadrophenia, also released the same year. Actor and musician Gary Shail had one of the leading roles in Quadrophenia and remembers his first meeting with Gary.

Gary Shail Photo © Gary Shail

GARY SHAIL : I first met Gary Holton on a cold and frosty night in the autumn of 1978 outside a pub in West London. I was there to shoot an integral scene for a movie called Quadrophenia, in which I played the character of the young mod, Spider. In the scene to be filmed that evening, I was to receive a severe beating from a gang of 'rockers' led by a particularly nasty specimen to be played by Mr Holton. Franc Roddam (director) introduced us and informed us that as per usual there would be a lot of hanging around, whilst all the lights and cameras were set up for the first shot.

Gary and I headed for the bar, closely followed by a beautiful dark-haired girl who turned out to be Gary's wife, Donna. They both looked like 'rock stars', and I liked them both immediately. I was only nineteen at the time and had never heard of Heavy Metal Kids, but when Gary told me he was the lead singer in the band, I was hardly surprised—he looked like the archetypal rock'n'roll front man, and he also drank like one. I liked him even more.

The filming went well, and once we had been cleared by Franc, it was about two in the morning. Gary and Donna lived in Maida Vale, which wasn't far from my West Hampstead flat, so we shared a cab, and on arrival at their place, they invited me in for a nightcap, which turned into breakfast drinks and then on to more drinks, once the local pub opened the following day. I knew we were going to be friends.

I became a regular visitor to Gary and Donna's little basement flat. I had my own band at the time and used to rehearse in a damp and smelly studio just around the corner in Maida Vale, so they would often visit and drag me back to theirs for the evening. Gary was always working on new music and lyric ideas that were often bizarre and hysterically funny. I loved the atmosphere he always created, and although he was often pissed and stoned, it never seemed to obscure his creativity in any way, except when he drank brandy (usually straight from the bottle), which seemed to depress him to the point of tears. He was frustrated with the music business, it seemed, and thought he had been treated badly by it. As far as he was concerned, he was a superstar! The only problem was, he was the only one who knew it.

In 1979, I had started recording an album with my own band in London's Marquee studios with a producer called Nick Tauber, who had also produced Thin Lizzy. Phil Lynott and Gary Moore were regular visitors to the studio and would sit in the control room on the mixing desk, whilst I, usually unsuccessfully, tried to get some work done. One night I happened to mention Gary's name, and the room fell silent. Unbeknown to me, Donna had been Gary Moore's long-term girlfriend and the love of his life. Gary Holton with his 'fucking cheeky cockney charm' had stolen her from under his nose and was going to pay for it. I didn't know—or particularly want to know—Gary Moore very well back then, but I was extremely glad it wasn't me he was looking for. It was years later when that I realised the girl pictured on Moore's debut album was Donna!

MATT DANGERFIELD : I really liked Gary. He was good company, although he never seemed to have any money at the time, so you ended up paying for him a lot. He did come along with The Boys for a few out-of-town gigs, but I think that was because he wasn't doing much at the time.

Photo © Matt Dangerfield

MATT DANGERFIELD : I only met Donna through Gary, although I'd seen her around previously with Thin Lizzie, etc. I had just split up with a long-term girlfriend when Donna latched on to me. She told me that she and Gary were no longer together (he was off on an acting tour—Once a Catholic, I think—at the time) and that he wouldn't care anyway. I don't know what the truth was, but our relationship didn't last long, and when I next met Gary back in London, he had a new girlfriend, Susan, and nothing was mentioned about Donna.

ALAN BUTCHER : I remember one time when Gary was looking for the man who was hanging out with his wife, Donna. He was at the 100 Club and did that trick of stabbing between his fingers as fast as he could on a table. I knew the man was Matt of The Boys, but I never told Gary

MAX SPLODGE : I was living over in Kent at one point, and Gary phoned me up one day. He was doing a play called Once a Catholic down in Richmond, and he phoned me up one day, and he said, "Er, I'm right up to my neck in shit and bullets." He said, "I couldn't come and stay with you for a while?" So when I told my girlfriend at the time Gary was coming to stay for a while, it didn't go down too well because she knew what the two of us were like together. So anyway, I told her that you have to help a mate out. So I waited for him, but I didn't hear anything from him, and he didn't turn up. I didn't hear anything the next day either. I couldn't get in touch with him, as we didn't have mobile phones in those days, obviously. It turned out that after he'd finished at the theatre, instead of coming over to me, he went to a casino he used to go to often, as he'd just got paid. Normally, he'd lose all his money within an hour. But that night, he met up with Susan Harrison, and from that day onwards, he was with her.

Chapter 7

From Lipservice to Holton/Steel

In late 1979 or early 1980, Gary's life was spiralling out of control again, and he wasn't in a good place, when he bumped into a familiar figure on the gigging circuit in London: Casino Steel. Gary was desperate to get off the drugs and clean himself up, even if it meant leaving London for a while to do so.

> *"I was a wreck. Gary was a wreck, so we agreed to escape together."*

CASINO STEEL : **I actually met Gary Holton when we were both playing a club in London called The Speakeasy. After that, we would bump into each other every now and then and became great mates. In 1980, we met in a pub and were both experiencing the same problems. We basically just wanted to get away from the circus. People were dying left, right and centre. We were both struggling with alcohol addictions, and he was into some drugs. I was a wreck. Gary was a wreck, so we agreed to escape together. I said I know some people in Norway. Let's go there and get away from all the craziness.**

Casino thought that if they could both leave London and live in Norway for a while, it would give them a chance to pull themselves together and get clean. Gary said Casino called leaving London 'running away'. Casino was an influential musician and had a lot of respect in the Norwegian music industry. They had to make a living in Norway, and Casino, who had been writing songs and performing most of his life, had the idea that they would punk-up old country-and-western covers.

In 1969, it was clear that there were large oil and gas reserves in the North Sea. The first oil field was Ekofisk, and it produced 427,442 barrels of crude in 1980. Suddenly, there was a multitude of jobs available on the oil rigs in the North Sea, and Casino, fascinated by this new pioneering industry, compared the oil workers to cowboys braving a new frontier. They were modern-day cowboys: hard-working, hard-drinking and hard-loving. The term 'Rigrock' was coined by Casino to describe his new music genre.

The first single, Ruby, a cover of the Kenny Rogers hit, Ruby, Don't Take Your Love to Town, was crudely made and sent to Casino's old bandmate from The Boys, Matt Dangerfield, in London. Drummer and close friend of Casino Steel, Geir Waade, was given the job of going to London to organise the first single where Gary would add the vocals. Travelling to London on his own wasn't tempting, so Geir asked his neighbour and fellow musician, Jon Petter Westerlund, to accompany him on a week's trip.

JON PETTER WESTERLUND : Geir Waade was going into the Berwick Street studios in Soho with Matt Dangerfield. The studio was downstairs in a basement. I went in with him and said hi to people, and Gary was there, so I said hi to him, too, as I'd never met him before. I hadn't met any of them before, except for Geir, obviously. I decided to go for a walk, as there was nothing for me to do in the studio. It was none of my business.

I had a walk around Soho for a couple of hours, and when I got back to the studio, there was a heavy atmosphere. Everyone looked very serious, and I sensed something was wrong, so I said cheerfully, "What the fuck's going on here then?" Geir answered there was a gap between the tracks that had been laid down in Nidaros Studios in Trondheim, Norway, and the stuff they had done at Berwick Street. Even after Gary had put the vocals on, it still wasn't working. There were several guitarists there, who had tried their hand at mixing it to make the sound good, but no one managed it. So Geir said, "Oi, Jon Petter, you're a guitarist, you try something." So I said, "What can I do that these guys can't?" And Geir answered in his thick Trondheim's dialect, "I dunno, play some guitar. We'll let the tape roll and you play, and we'll see what we get."

So I got stuck in and did a bit, and they suddenly stopped the tape and said, "Fucking hell, that was good! Can you play it like that all the way through?" I seriously thought they were taking the piss because I didn't know what I'd done that was so good. They were practically calling me a genius, and when the song was over and done with, they came to shake my hand. This was the first single to be made. I thought they were making fun of me, but after a while I realised that they actually meant it.

We were invited to a party that same night, and people came forward to shake my hand. I felt a bit embarrassed. Gary said, "You really need to be a part of this." So when I got back to Trondheim, I was asked to go into Nidaros Studios and play guitar in the same style on all the other tracks they had done. One of these was Irene Goodnight.

> **"It ended up being banned by the BBC because of the 'crazy Irish war' reference in the lyrics."**

MATT DANGERFIELD : I only properly met Gary when Geir Waade brought over a two-inch master tape of Ruby that he had been working on with Cas and some session musicians back in Trondheim. His idea was to add some guitars and get Gary to sing the lead vocal and asked me to help out.

I had booked Berwick street studios for him, and when we put the tape on the machine, I thought it was terrible. It was pretty much a straight cover of the Kenny Rogers version with wimpy shuffle drums, girly backing vocals and pedal-steel doodling-about all over it. Worst of all, it had no snare backbeat to make it rock.

It needed a lot of sorting out, so basically I ended up producing the track. As we didn't have a snare, we added handclaps as the backbeat, put on some power chords and added the guitar licks to cover/beef up the girl vocals on the chorus.

Then Gary arrived to sing the vocal, and the track turned out great. We even got a single release for it the next day with Safari Records, whom I was signed to at the time, although it ended up being banned by the BBC because of the 'crazy Irish war' reference in the lyrics.

After the recording, I went for a drink with Gary, and we became good friends and saw each other quite a lot from then on.

Gary thought Jon Petter Westerlund's name too long and that it felt like tongue aerobics. He said it wouldn't go down well in the UK, and they wanted to shorten it: his name, not his tongue. Casino suggested some exotic varieties like Westhausen, but Gary was having none of it. It was finally agreed that Jon Petter Westerlund would thereafter be known as J P West. It was a name that would stick with him for a huge chunk of his musical career.

J P WEST : **Gary came to Trondheim during the spring of 1980 to put vocals onto the other tracks. He came to Trondheim with his wife, a pretty dark-haired girl called Donna. The time they spent in Trondheim was quite strange because they fought all the time. We'd take them out in the evening, and we had to make sure we got them back to the hotel separately, or they would be bickering and squabbling and fighting. They seemed to have a very stormy relationship.**

Anyway, we all went back to London to make videos for several songs, including Irene Goodnight. We were in Saville Row, and we got our hair done. We were in the studio and had some PR photos taken, and there was one in the Norwegian magazine Det Nye of the new band Lipservice, which is what we called ourselves to begin with.

It was just the four of us: I was on guitar, Gary sang, Geir Waade on drums and Casino Steel on keyboard and vocal. The Norwegian record producer, Bjørn Nessjø, played bass on the record, but he wasn't in the band. We were supposed to practice, and we needed a proper full-time bassist. A mate of mine from my home town, Horten, Roald Villesvik, joined us and moved to Trondheim.

It was at this point I met Gary properly for the first time at Skansen Disco. He was only in Norway for a couple of weeks the first time, when he came with his wife, Donna.

After that he came back on his own. After I met him at Skansen, I would bump into him regularly at a café called Daniel, which was the daytime meeting place for our friends. Gary and I would often find ourselves having long conversations about his life and mine.

Most Norwegians at the time weren't fantastically fluent in English, and Gary said he liked to talk to me because he didn't have to explain himself all the time. I knew what he meant straightaway, and although I'm a dreadful chatterbox, I like to think I can also be entertaining. I think Gary felt talking to me was okay because he didn't have to be charming or flirty. We established from the outset that wasn't on the menu, so it was easy to chill and chat.

> **"Marith and I were asked to do backing vocals. We sang like two seagulls down a tip, but we didn't tell them that."**

One Friday night, my best friend, Marith, and I were out at the night club called Down Town, trying to have a good time. It wasn't really hopping, and we were pretty bored, when there was a call for Marith at the bar. There was a telephone call for her from the record producer, Bjørn Nessjø. Bjørn was in Nidaros Studios just outside Trondheim, and they were working on the Lipservice single, Irene Goodnight. They had decided they wanted a pub sing-along feel to it and wondered whether Marith and I would be willing to get a taxi to the studio to help out with backing vocals.

FAST LIVING

Lipservice facsimile from Det Nye magazine 1980.
Geir Waade, JP West, Casino Steel and Gary Holton

Bjørn said they were having a party, so we were to take some extra booze from the bar and go as soon as possible. They would pay for everything. It wasn't something we would normally have considered doing, since neither Marith nor I can sing.

Marith and I were both really dreadful singers; we sounded like two seagulls down a tip. We didn't tell Bjørn this, as the offer sounded exciting, and there wasn't anything else happening at the club. We agreed if 'push came to shove', we would mime. We were certain we would get away with it.

We got a taxi to Nidaros and were met by Bjørn, Casino and Gary at the door. They took the booze, and I saw that there was a long table and some chairs in one of the larger recording rooms. On the table there was lots of beer. They added the beer and wine we had taken along and told us to sit down. We arrived at about eleven p.m. and lots of people were turning up from all over. Some sober, some drunk. Gary seemed sober and in high spirits. J P West was there. Marith and I were the only girls. The others they had managed to round up were guys, mostly musicians, who weren't gigging that night. We soon realised this was a spur-of-the-moment idea.

Gary took a bottle of lukewarm beer from the table, as the room was filled with the country-and-western song Irene Goodnight. Gary sang the verse, and we sang the chorus. I couldn't hear my own voice, so Marith and I just sang along with everyone else. There was one moment when I saw Bjørn and Casino and the studio technician roar with laughter, but because everything was so loud, I was sure they couldn't hear my voice catwauling above the rest. Well, as it turned out, I was standing next to the microphone, so I'm pretty sure I was the reason for their amusement.

After many takes, the room we were in was getting pretty hot. More beer was brought in, and by the time we were finished, it was three a.m. in the morning. Everyone was the worse for wear. Irene Goodnight rang in my ears so much, I couldn't get to sleep when I got home. I swear I can hear myself on the record, out of tune and really loud. This was my and Marith's only time doing backing vocals, and they never invited us back, strangely enough. The next day we couldn't speak, having lost our voices after the singing. When I laughed, I sounded like a donkey with asthma for the best part of the following week.

J P WEST : I remember when we did Irene Goodnight in the studio late at night and had a wicked party.

Gary returned to London after a couple of weeks, but would soon return for a longer stay. I will always remember him arriving at the café after he'd been away for a while. He would be in a great mood and greet everyone heartily as he entered. He was always the centre of attention, and that's the way he liked it.

"Hiya, darling. You all right? Did ya' miss me?" he would sometimes say, cheekily.

"No, hardly noticed you were gone," would be my standard reply, and it would make him laugh.

J P WEST : The first thing we did in London was to make a video for Irene Goodnight. We went to Camden, to a place just across the road from Dingwalls. We also made a video for Casino's other band, The Hollywood Brats, at Dingwalls. Gary was seeing a pretty blonde girl called Susan Harrison now, and she was in all the

subsequent videos that were made for the band. I don't know what happened with Donna. I didn't ask.

There was a pub across the road, and we asked the owner if we could use it for a video shoot. We'd get people in off the street and pay for their beer. So we offered people on the street free beer to be in the video. It was a lot of fun. Unfortunately, someone had made a deal for the making of the video, which was under the legal minimum charge, so there was a problem with it being shown on TV in the UK. The song Ruby was also boycotted because Gary changed the words to make it his own and sang 'crazy Irish war', but that was later. Irene Goodnight was first.

We went back and forth to London about three times in all, I believe. On one trip to London, we were invited to Matt Dangerfield's apartment in Maida Vale. It was a basement apartment and a pretty gloomy place with black walls. Matt was dating the model Jane Hargrave at the time. She is the most beautiful woman in the world. I was totally star-struck. I'd seen photos of her naked in Penthouse Magazine, and here she was in the flesh. I didn't know where to look. I was a bit embarrassed but dead impressed.

"I thought, shite, I'm going to get my face punched in."

Gary was in Trondheim in the summer of 1980 for a longer spell. The music he was doing with Casino hadn't really taken off, and he needed something to do whilst he was waiting for something to happen with Lipservice that would make him some money. It was decided that he would front the local band, Vikings, on tour and local gigs.

DAG RASMUSSEN : The first time I met Gary Holton was in Trondheim in 1980. I think it was at a café/bar place called Daniel. I was playing in a band called Vikings, and I was there with another band member, Åge Haugan. Gary had been in Norway for a short while, and before the Holton/Steel tour was going to happen, it had been decided that Gary would play with Vikings for a while. I think it was supposed to be for six months to a year.

The first thing Gary said to me when he met me was—well, he's an Englishman—so he greeted me ever so politely, and then when he thought I couldn't hear him, he asked Åge whether I could really play the drums. I was very young at the time—seventeen—and I'm not a big guy, but then neither was he. He thought I looked like a child, a Boy Scout or choirboy.

Anyway, we went up to Nidaros Studios and did a couple of takes of some material he had brought with him, and in the middle of one, he just got up and left the mic. He came storming into the drum booth. I thought, "Shite, I'm going to get my face punched in," because he looked a bit wild. So he rushed over to me as I was sitting behind my drum set, and he picked me up. He lifted me up from my seat and placed a kiss on each cheek and said, "Now we can continue." I was quite shocked but remember being happy that perhaps he was pleased with my drumming, after all.

Viking was the first professional band I was in. I joined them straight after finishing college. I'm not sure how the deal with playing with Gary came about, but I think perhaps Åge met Gary through Casino Steel whilst on holiday in the UK.

Gary was working with Casino Steel on the singles and the first album with the rigrock band Lipservice and gigging at the weekends with Vikings. He would go back to London every few weeks or so.

Gary looked and acted very differently to other Norwegian boys at the time, with the exception of Casino Steel and Geir Waade perhaps. He played the role of the rock-musician superstar well, and it suited him. His personality was so charismatic, I don't think there was anyone around at the time who ever doubted he would become something big at some point. The gigs he played were rife with groupies, but I think they had merely become a fact of life for Gary.

DAG RASMUSSEN : Gary had to make a living, and playing with us was a good way of doing that. We went on tour together. The first tour was to places in southern Norway. We were gone for at least three weeks. Gary drank a lot and kept popping pills, but I became very fond of him because he was just such a really all-right guy. He was caring towards others. Gary and I used to share a hotel room for most of the tour. I certainly noticed then how much he liked the ladies.

There's a really funny episode I remember from the tour, when we were in Ålesund on the west coast of Norway. We'd played the gig, and there was a captain on a fishing trawler from Hitra, (small rural island off the coast of Trondheim). He'd just bought himself a new fishing-trawler and it was in the Ålesund docks. It was a lovely, great big, new, shiny trawler.

The captain invited us back to his trawler for food and drinks, the works. He was a really nice captain. He proudly gave us a tour of his boat, and when we got up to the bridge, Mr Holton decided to play silly beggar

and started pressing all the buttons and flicking switches on the control panel. He hit anything he could see, and the boat sprung to life and sounded like it was going to take off right out of the water.

Gary was pissed as a newt, to put it mildly. He lay there on the bridge, shouting to the captain, "Captain, Captain, take me to the high seas. I'll pay you whatever it takes!" I could see the captain sincerely regretted inviting us. He threw himself at the control panel and ran from one side to another turning off the engine, whilst the rest of the band laughed so hard we couldn't breathe. Needless to say, we were put on land again straightaway.

So then we're walking back to the Parken hotel, and Gary manages to pick up some bird on the way back. Well, he and I were sharing a room, as usual, and I thought, "Shit, this isn't nice." Anyway, when we got back to the room, I went to bed and placed myself at the far end of the bed, as close to the wall as I could possibly get in the double bed and kept thinking, "Bollocks, you're not doing this to me. I'm your friend," but of course, he just carried on. I couldn't sleep, but I shut my eyes firmly and tried to ignore them, and suddenly Gary pushed my shoulder, "Oi, Dag, Dag, have you got a cigarette?"

Gary could be black or white. One minute he would be very happy, and then he might become a bit melancholy and sad too. Whilst we were in Ålesund, he got a message that a friend of his in England had died. I can't remember who it was, but a well-known musician or actor, and he was really unhappy. He grieved for his friend.

Towards the end of the summer of 1980, Gary told me that his girlfriend, Susan Harrison, would be visiting him in Norway. He seemed excited by the prospect, and I know he was looking forward to it a lot. What I came to realise about Gary was that he did actually love Susan a great deal, but he was never in a relationship in the traditional way. He wasn't unfaithful in his mind, he just did what he wanted to, when he wanted to, and he loved pretty girls. However, when Susan was around, he only had eyes for her.

DAG RASMUSSEN : I only met his girlfriend, Susan, once—a beautiful lady from London. We were in Oslo and playing the club called Ridderhallen. That was the first time I met her. I remember thinking, 'It can't be easy being Gary Holton's girlfriend.' I think it would have been a challenge for any girl. I don't think he meant to do stuff, you know chase skirt, but I think he just didn't think it through. He was just like that. He didn't really think his actions had consequences.

Susan arrived in Trondheim one sunny day towards the end of summer. Gary was proudly parading her around, and they wandered into a restaurant where I was having lunch. A few weeks before she arrived, he had asked me whether I would like to meet her, and I replied that yes, I would love to. When they walked in, I was immediately struck by how beautiful she was. She was a slim blonde—eighties' rock-chic girlfriend. Gary brought her straight over to my table, where I was having lunch with a few friends, and they sat down. My second impression of Susan was that she was sullen and not enjoying her time in Norway. She had only been in Norway for a couple of days. I could see Gary was a little worried, too. I got a vibe there was something going on, and I couldn't put my finger on it at first.

Gary talked to my friends, and Susan didn't say a word. She took my hand when Gary introduced me but hardly offered me a glance. It was like she was trying to stay aloof and keep her distance and doing her best to look bored. I decided to try to get her to talk, and I asked her about her trip up from Oslo in the band van and how long she was going to stay. It wasn't long before she started to talk to me. After a few minutes into the conversation, I excused myself, as I needed the ladies', and I turned to Susan and asked her whether she did too. In those days, girls used going to the loo together to be able to talk about the guys without them hearing our conversation. Susan said yes and off we went.

I soon learned that Susan was very well aware of all the local girls hanging around Gary and the groupies, who regularly followed a pop group or other celebrity in the hope of having a sexual relationship with them.

She told me they weren't shy, and they didn't seem to care that he had his girlfriend with him. She said she was used to it from the gigs in the UK, but the difference in Norway was that she couldn't communicate with the girls. They would be speaking in Norwegian and freezing her out of the conversation, and she wasn't enjoying it. She said that Casino and a few others were very nice to her, but none of the local girls would talk to her at all. Gary was off doing his studio stuff and gigging, and she was starting to feel a little isolated.

When we got back to the table and our lunch, Susan and I had decided that the guys could go off to do their rock-star stuff at the gig that night, and Susan and I were going out to the Hawk Club, Trondheim's trendiest club for the over-eighteens. I could see Gary was pleased, and he knew I would never tell Susan anything about what had been going on with him in Trondheim that might upset her. I lost count of Gary's ladies, and they never lasted long anyway. It was nice to see him with Susan and to see how he acted when he truly cared about someone.

J P WEST : I was a good friend of Gary's. I met Susan, who was his girlfriend at the time, and I visited them at their home in London. I actually have Gary to thank for keeping away from drug use. We were at a party in London, and he took me aside. He said, "You can smoke all the weed you like, sniff your nose full of coke, but never, never touch heroin." His warning really struck a chord, and I've never touched anything.

Susan stayed in Trondheim for about a week, perhaps two weeks at the most. She had a son who was staying with someone in London, and although she was enjoying spending time with Gary, she was missing her little boy and wanted to go back. We wrote to each other from time to time after that, but then we lost touch.

DAG RASSMUSSEN : Later, on another tour, we were playing the north of Norway in a rural area in a town called Alta, we had a razzia by the police. It was after the gig, and suddenly there were dogs and police in the hotel rooms. We were all forced to wait in the hall in our underwear. I was scared shitless for Gary, because I knew what he was up to with drugs. I was old enough to understand he was dabbling with things that weren't legal. The police didn't find anything on any of us. I've no idea who could have tipped the police off about us, but somebody did. I was just happy they didn't find anything and we could go back to bed again.

The line-up of Lipservice varied as the months went by without them making any impact on the Norwegian music scene. J P West left Trondheim to play with a Danish band. His friend, Roald, also left. I remember that there was some unease in the band. This didn't involve J P or Roald, but someone outside the band had spread some vindictive rumours. There was a lot of speculation about who had tipped off the police that they might find drugs on the band in Alta. Casino was livid, and I think he secretly suspected who it might have been, but being a very level-headed person, he didn't take it any further. I believe he wanted to get his music out, and petty jealousy wasn't something he tolerated.

J P WEST: Casino was trying to sell the music and the concept to record companies all the time. It wasn't until late 1980 or very early 1981, when he attended MIDEM (Marché International du Disque et de l'Edition Musicale) in Cannes that anyone showed any interest. He was told that bands were not the thing anymore, and single artists were the up-and-coming trend. So they suggested that to be successful it had to be just Gary Holton. As it was Casino's project to begin with, he wasn't having any of it, and they finally agreed it would be known as Holton/Steel. I was playing in another band by this time, and moved to Denmark, where I stayed for ten years.

Lipservice was being managed by a company called Continental Records, owned by a Norwegian guy with a very English sounding name—Barry Matheson. Barry was the money behind Lipservice, and when it was decided that Lipservice was to disband and Holton/Steel to form, Barry had the job of explaining this to the remaining two members of Lipservice.

"There didn't seem to be much interest in Lipservice."

J P WEST : In February 1981, Geir Waade and I were called in to a meeting with Barry Matheson. He owned Continental Records, with whom Lipservice had a contract. It was a fantastic contract. We each got ten percent royalties each. There were four of us and a contract giving away forty percent royalties was unheard of.

Anyway, at the meeting, Geir and I were told that there didn't seem to be much interest in the Lipservice record. No one had wanted to buy the rights to it during all the time they had been trying to get it out. We were told there was someone interested, but only as a solo project for Holton and Steel, and Barry wanted to sign us out of the contract. I think we were paid the equivalent of three hundred pounds in compensation and promised another five hundred pounds should the album ever be released.

In the contract it stated that should there be, against all odds, a hit in the future, the remaining band members (Gary and Casino) had a moral obligation to provide us with additional compensation for our work. If we didn't sign the contract, the alternative was to take on a quarter of the debt, which at the time was about 800,000 Norwegian kroner. This is a lot of money. It had been used to cover recording studio, videos and travel. I wasn't really keen to have a 200,000-kroner debt, with no prospect of the record ever making any money. As I remember, Barry made a good job of persuading us to sign the release form.

MAX SPLODGE: I remember when I used to go and see Gary—he had a band called The Gems. Then he had another project—a band called Lipservice. I remember him turning up when I was doing Top of the Pops in 1980. I had a hit with Two Pints of Lager and a Packet of Crisps, and he turned up with his girlfriend, Sue. He gave me and my girlfriend a t-shirt each with Lipservice printed on it. I didn't understand what it was for, and he said, "It's my new band." Then it was called Holton/Steel, so I never understood what the Lipservice was about.

Gary was travelling back and forth to London but still spending most of his time in Norway. He would always be in the cafés and restaurants that we used to frequent for lunch, when he wasn't away on tour. I personally think Gary was getting a little lonely in Norway, and his hopes that anything would come of the Holton/Steel partnership were diminishing day by day.

MARITH : I remember bumping into Gary one day, and he remarked that he was sick of eating in restaurants all the time. As I was on my way home and my dad was making dinner, I invited him to join us. He accepted the offer eagerly. We had Joika (meatballs made from reindeer meat in a creamy sauce—a speciality from Lapland) and potatoes. Gary loved it, but he but he was disappointed not to have any wine with the meal. Afterwards, he thanked us for dinner and said the food was good, but dinner without wine was like a shower without water. Ungrateful sod. Funny though.

One day, during late autumn of 1980, I met Gary at a local café. He looked like his usual self but told me he was getting antsy and was starting to reconsider his time in Norway. He missed London and told me he had just had some bad news. He had been invited to audition for the lead of the Australian heavy-metal band ACDC earlier that year. They had lost their singer, Bon Scott, in February 1980. Gary told me it was a foregone conclusion that he would get the job and that they really wanted him as their new lead vocal and front. He said he thought it was just a matter of turning up, and he could say goodbye to Norway and move on to greener pastures. When he was told the date for the audition in London, he said it felt like a 'sign from above'. I seem to remember the date of the audition being Bon Scott's birthday, but I'm not sure.

Gary was very positive about playing with ACDC and excited about the audition. He decided that since the audition date was so significant, he brought a whole crate of whiskey—or perhaps it was brandy—with him. I had never heard of ACDC, but Gary said it was the previous singer's preferred tipple. Gary had been partying hard the night before and was a few minutes late for the audition. He told me how he walked in all cocky and sure of himself and put the crate down and opened a bottle to share with everyone. He said there was total silence. Nobody took anything to drink, and nobody said anything for a long time. He thought he had done something wrong, but he couldn't work out what. He was informed a few days later that although ACDC thought he was a good candidate for the job, Bon Scott had died of alcohol poisoning, and the last thing the band wanted was to have another alcoholic as front man. The job went to ex-Geordie singer Brian Johnson. Gary was devastated and felt very foolish. The fact that the next ACDC album, Back in Black, was released that year and was an instant mega hit, reminded him of his situation in Norway and not getting anywhere with his career at the time.

J P WEST : In August 1981, Ruby was released as a single and became an instant hit. It was number one in the Norwegian charts from August and until Christmas. I played guitar on the first album and on a few of the tracks on the second album that was now Holton/Steel. They called it Rigrock, and it was all Casino's idea from the start. Nevertheless, I haven't seen any of that 'obligatory compensation' after the record was a big hit in Scandinavia.

Holton/Steel's single release of Ruby was played everywhere. Suddenly Casino and Gary were a success, and the music that no one thought would ever come to anything was number one in the charts for weeks and weeks. The video accompanying the single featured Susan Harrison as Casino's girlfriend in a bar. The earlier Lipservice video wasn't used. Suddenly things were moving in the right direction, and the first album, Gary Holton & Casino Steel was released on Polydor Records, featuring Susan as a blonde in a bar. Gary and Cas were on the uptown bus and very happy about it.

DAG RASMUSSEN : I would regularly see Gary around in Trondheim and in the music scene. There weren't that many of us around who made a living from our music and had days off. I remember him being very humble about it all when the Holton/Steel collaboration was a huge success.

DAG RASMUSSEN : Actually, when the success was a fact, and radio, TV and the rest of the media threw themselves over Gary and Casino, I thought they just took it all in their stride and were humble. I'm sure they could be cocky from time to time, because I've seen that side, too, but it never meant anything—do you know what I mean? They were just nice to everyone.

Suddenly, everyone wanted a part of Holton/Steel. Ruby was a smash hit, and the album that came later was practically ripped off the music shops' shelves. Gary and Casino, who had run away from London to get away from the craziness, found themselves in an even worse situation than before.

CASINO STEEL : I'd said to Gary, "Let's go to Norway and get away from all the craziness." Then we had a huge success with our first album in Norway, and it led to things getting crazier than ever. So escaping didn't work. We basically just moved the craziness over to Trondheim, Norway.

Holton/Steel went on a tour of Norway, and the second album was soon ready for release the following year. Susan, Gary's girlfriend, would appear on several videos. The next album was called Holton & Steel Part II and featured Susan in a maid's uniform. This album was not as successful as the first, but Holton & Steel continued work on a third album.

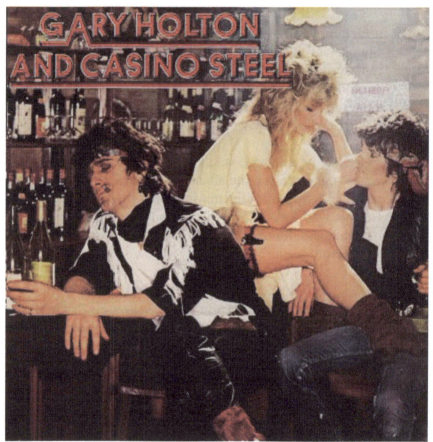

Album cover. Gary Holton, Susan Harrison and Casino Steel

Holton/Steel on tour, Torstein Flakne on guitar © Arne Olav Nordtømme

DAG RASMUSSEN : I was in Stavanger, another town on the west coast of Norway, when the first Holton/Steel tour started. I'd left Vikings and was playing with the Four Jets. We were set to gig Sjøhuset the following day, and we arrived a day early just to go to the Holton/Steel gig. We weren't seated very near to the stage at all, but further towards the back of the room. Gary suddenly saw me, possibly because my hair is very blonde, and he came over to our table with his mic and jumped on to the table. He crawled over to where I was sitting, and started kissing my face shouting, "Dag, my friend for eternity!" And then he wanted me to duet Irene Goodnight with him. I'm no singer—I'm a drummer—but it was really good fun, and that's just the type of guy he was.

Later, I remember I met them at the nightclub called Down Town, in Oslo. This was what was known as a key-club back in the early eighties. It was a club where you had to have a key to get in. They would hand out keys to musicians, artists, celebrities, sports stars—you get the gist. The keys were in different colours, depending on where in the hierarchy you were. Anyway, I was given a key. When it was handed to me, Gary and Casino Steel were present. I can't remember what colour my key was, but I was very pleased, and I politely put my hand out to shake and thanked the guy. So there I was saying, "Thank you so very much for the key. That's really kind of you." And Casino interrupted and said, "Hey, Dag, what the fuck do you think you're doing? You can't thank these people for that key!" I didn't know what he meant. So I told him that I'd been taught to say thank you when someone gives me something. It's called 'manners'. Casino answered, "You can't thank them. You're a pop star. You should take it for granted, and you're looking foolish for thanking them." Oh well, I suppose they're used to this cocky attitude in England, where I'm sure it's more common to take things like that for granted, but I'd prefer to be polite. With hindsight, Cas might have been pulling my leg, for all I know.

After the initial success of the first single, followed by the album, Holton/Steel promptly went on a two-week tour of Norway. The music style seemed to appeal to the Norwegian public, and the tour was a huge success. The rest of the band changed depending on who was available to play. One such person was Steinar Krogstad, drummer from Trondheim and long-time friend of Casino Steel.

STEINAR KROGSTAD : I can't remember all that much about it, as I was only twenty years old at the time, and I only did a little of the drumming with them. I did the second album and, I think, maybe a bit of the third. I was on the Norway tour, which was a lot of fun.
We then went on to play a couple of gigs in London. I was told it was just to see what sort of a turn-out we would get. I can't remember the first venue, but the second was the old Marquee Club. As I recall, the turn-out wasn't all that good.

MAX SPLODGE : I went to see Gary when they played the gig at the Marquee Club with the Holton/Steel thingy. It was good to see him, but it was quite a brief meeting because they left London right after the gig. I think they were flying straight back to Norway.

FAST LIVING

STEINAR KROGSTAD : **We played the Marquee Club as the last gig of two and had to leave straight afterwards. We actually flew in and flew out in a private plane. It wasn't us trying to act like pop stars—it was out of necessity, because of the time frame. We left the Marquee and went straight to the airport and caught the last flight of the day.**

Holton/Steel released several albums together. The second was aptly Holton/Steel Part II, released in 1982, and the third, Holton/Steel Third Edition, was released the following year in 1983. None of the albums were to become as popular as the first. Gary had started to get bored with his time in Norway and was now spending more and more time with Susan in London.

Casino contacted his old bandmate from The Boys, guitarist and songwriter Honest John Plain, to go over to Norway to play with them. That might have been a very bad decision, as Honest John Plain and Gary soon became partners in crime and would skive off and hide from Casino, when they should have been at rehearsals or in the studio.

I remember meeting Honest John Plain in a pub in Trondheim. It was late afternoon, and he looked as if he had just woken up. He was carrying a very snappy-looking suit that he was going to sell to a local musician, as he needed the cash. We sat talking together and Gary arrived. The bartender at this particular pub was another English guy called Mike. He had fallen in love with a pretty blonde Norwegian girl, who played a small role in one of the videos that was made for one of Holton/Steel's albums. Honest John Plain and Gary were having a beer and laughing at the previous nights' escapades, when they both suddenly got up and made a rush for the bar. Mike had alerted them that Bjørn Nessjø was parking his car on the street, right outside the bar. They were let out through the back door, leaving their half-empty beer glasses on the table and Gary's smouldering cigarette in the ashtray. Gary pointed a finger at me before he left and said, "You haven't seen us. We weren't here, okay?" I nodded and they scrambled for the back door, just as Casino Steel and Bjørn Nessjø entered the pub.

The first thing Casino asked everyone around the table was whether anyone had seen John or Gary. There was an awkward silence for a while, and nobody said anything. We all looked guiltily at the smouldering cigarette in the ashtray, wondering whether we would get into trouble with Casino if we were found out. We shook our heads—no, we hadn't seen them. At that moment I remember feeling really bad for Casino, as his music and the success they had was important to him, and Gary's behaviour was typical when he became bored with something. He would play games and run away. Everything was a joke to him, and he didn't take anything seriously. It was part of his charm, but I can see with hindsight that it can't have been easy to work with him sometimes.

HONEST JOHN PLAIN : Casino had already left the band (The Boys) in 1980 to team up with Gary Holton. Safari Records decided to drop us in 1981, when Boys Only bombed, and then Duncan (Reid, bass) left, so we decided to call it a day. We played a few more gigs in Italy, New York and Spain after we'd decided to finish, and those were great fun.

I had a great time with Holton/Steel and loved their music. Well, Gary was sort of out of control at that time, and I actually saved his life twice! We got on well and loved to have a few drinks and do other things together!

FAST LIVING

Unfortunately, no one dared to say anything to Gary when he turned up late or was incapacitated, so they needed a scapegoat. I was in the firing line, so I had to go.

When Honest John Plain left Holton/Steel, it was pretty much over. Gary did return to Norway, even after he was playing Wayne in Auf Wiedersehen, Pet. They made a song about it and got together for another album in 1984, titled Nr 4. Gary and Casino were firm friends, despite Gary's misbehaviour, and Casino visited him on numerous occasions in London. On one of these trips, after the Holton/Steel success, Gary introduced Casino to one of his old friends: Ronnie Wood (The Faces, The Rolling Stones). Ronnie and Gary had a mutual friend in Charlotte, the Swiss heiress, and had bumped into each other many times at her home. Ronnie made a sketch of Gary and Casino, which was used as promotion for the duo.

Gary was living in London now and spending more time on his acting than his singing, and his musical success in Norway went largely unnoticed in the UK.

Sketch of Gary Holton and Casino Steel by Ronnie Wood in 1983

Chapter 8

Fame and Fortune

When Gary moved back to London permanently in 1983, he and Susan lived in a flat in Ealing with Susan's young son, Max, from her marriage to singer Lulu's brother. Max was born in 1979. Gary kept going back to Norway from time to time to do music projects with Casino Steel, but he was spending most of his time in London with Sue and Max. Gary was doing commercials and theatre work to keep the wolves from the door but still had time for old mates like Max Splodge.

MAX SPLODGE : I was round at his house in Ealing. Susan had gone to bed, and I said, "I want to get another band together." And he said, "Yeah, you can still do your funny stuff and your punk stuff, but get a good rock band behind you." I said, "Yeah. Okay. I'll look into that." Then we had a few beers together and he said, "Hang on, I've got an idea. What do you reckon about this?" and he played me a tape of him singing three songs. He'd recorded it with a band from Yarmouth, which was originally a punk band called The Crabs. They were a bunch of young lads, whom I thought were excellent, and he suggested I tried them. At one point he was considering joining them, but he went with Heavy Metal Kids instead. I phoned them up, and they became my band. In fact, the guitarist is still with me now, thirty-odd years later.

When he came back from Norway, I used to see him all the time and we'd go off to the odd party. He even started to produce my first album. We were going off on our first tour, and I asked Gary if he could go down to the studio, called The Workhouse, down in the Old Kent Road, and finish mixing it for me. Unfortunately, at the time he was doing a play down in Brighton. He would come back and get to the studio at one in the morning, a bit worse for wear. And on the second night, he knocked a whole bottle of vodka over the mixing desk, so they refused to let him in any more. That was normal behaviour for him.

Gary, Susan and her son Max moved from Ealing to Maida Vale, just down the road from the Warrington pub and just around the corner from ex-Sex Pistols bassist Glen Matlock.

GLEN MATLOCK : Gary was living in Maida Vale when he got back from Norway, before the TV series. I used to know his missus, Sue. It was actually her that got him the gig at Auf Wiedersehen, Pet because she knew the writers. He was struggling a bit, and she kinda pushed to get him in it. They used to rehearse in a little church hall in Maida Vale, near where we lived. They'd be in the pub come half past eleven in the morning.

MIKE QUINN : I met Gary in London when he was doing Pump Boys and Dinettes, with Paul Jones. We linked up, and went clubbing at Stringfellows. Gary was quite outrageous. I remember, at the time, I used to wear my hair combed across, and Gary said, "Nah, nah, Mike, you want to comb your hair right back." This was 1984, and he was talking to people around us saying,

"Wouldn't he look better with his hair combed back?" Gary was like that, and I was saying, "Shut up!" Gary was involving other people in our conversation, whom we didn't even know. But Gary was outrageously funny. And he said, "Tomorrow I'm going to take you to the hairdresser." And he did, and he told the hairdresser how he should cut my hair. I just went along with it because I just thought it was funny. Gary had a whole entourage around him, and talked a lot about Heavy Metal Kids. All his entourage thought he was wonderful, and I did too, because he was that kind of guy.

GARY SHAIL : I didn't see much of Gary for a couple of years after 1979. I was on tour for much of the time and away from London. Of course, with no mobile telephones or internet, 'social networking' actually meant meeting and talking to 'real people' in person. Weird, eh? What was even weirder was being asked to star in London Weekend Television's new children's TV sitcom, Metal Mickey. The show was a surprise hit, regularly attracting twelve million viewers a week and making me a 'teenage pin-up' into the bargain, although in reality, I was in my early twenties.

Gary Holton had also been a busy lad. Doing that tiny part in Quadrophenia had paid dividends for him, as Franc Roddam, who had devised a new show about British builders working in Germany, introduced Gary to the writer Ian Le Frenais, who succumbed to Gary's "fucking cheeky cockney charm" and cast him as the loveable rogue, Wayne. The show, called Auf Weidersehen, Pet, was a massive hit, so now we were both TV stars.

The first series of Auf Wiedersehen, Pet, was aired in 1983. Wayne was a cockney carpenter who liked his drink, women and music, in that order, not unlike Gary himself. Those who knew Gary would say, carpentry apart, he was just playing himself. Wayne described himself as a bit of a Jack the Lad, who was very proud of his cockney roots and establishes himself as the group's expert of ladies.

The first series was broadcast on ITV in 1983 and was a huge hit. Auf Wiedersehen, Pet was about seven out-of-work men, screwed by the system, who got jobs as construction workers on a building site in Dusseldorf, West Germany. It focused on three men from Newcastle, making their way to Germany after saying goodbye ('auf wiedersehen' in German) to their wives. Although they had been promised hostel accommodation, the men found themselves living together in a hut reminiscent of POW accommodation, and the series followed their friendship and work. Over the course of thirteen episodes, the 'Magnificent Seven' delighted the whole nation with comic and romantic adventures, and the first series ended when a change in German tax laws forced them to return home to England.

The series was rehearsed in a church hall in Maida Vale, and the building site used for filming was a lot at the back of Elstree Studios in Hertfordshire, where they now make Eastenders. Such was their attention to detail, they had thousands of bricks imported to the UK from West Germany as they were slightly larger than the ones used on British building sites.

GLEN MATLOCK : Gary Holton was funny. He used to live around the corner from me. They used to rehearse in a nearby church hall that was just around the corner and then go on to a pub. Gary lived close to a

big pub called The Warrington. I used to watch Auf Wiedersehen, Pet when it was really popular in the UK, and then I'd go to that pub. Gary would do the same, but as he lived closer to it than me, he would already be there, wearing the same clothes he wore in the episode we'd just seen, accepting drinks from everyone. (laughs). He was cheeky.

Facsimile from Auf Wiedersehen, Pet promotion

Gary's role in Auf Wiedersehen, Pet made him instantly famous in the UK, and he was on his best behaviour again for the first series. 1983 marked another happy occasion in Gary's life with the birth of his and Susan's son, Red. Gary suddenly seemed to have everything he ever wanted. He was a famous actor getting recognition for his talent. He had a beautiful girlfriend, a son and Susan's son, Max. Gary was making money doing what he did best: entertaining people. Things in his life were good in many ways.

RONNIE THOMAS : **In 1980, I buggered off to Australia. I'd had enough of this country and Thatcherism, and I had a lot of money. I'd just written a song for a band Keith (Boyce) had joined—Bram Tchaikovsky. I wrote a song for them called Girl of my Dreams. That took off in America, and I think it sold nearly half a million. That's not bad for a brand new band and their first single. So I got a bit of money from that. Nothing much was happening. The band (Heavy Metal Kids) had split up.**

KEITH BOYCE : **I joined Bram Tchaikovsky in London. Bram was from a band called The Motors. The Motors wanted me to be their drummer, but I turned them down, as I was still with Heavy Metal Kids. I regretted it not long after, as they had two top-ten hits straightaway! So then Bram, the guitarist, asked me to do some gigs with him and a mate of his on bass. I did, and within a few weeks we had every record company in London bidding on us, I think mainly because Bram was still in The Motors. Anyway we signed a big deal, and within six weeks of playing together, we were soon in the studio. We didn't have enough songs for the album, so I suggested we do some of Ron's songs. We**

did two, which both went on the album, and the record company picked one of them, Girl Of My Dreams, as the single. The album and single went into the American charts, and both reached the top thirty.

RONNIE THOMAS : I got back to England in 1984, and I was staying over at a friend's flat in Clapham. I was talking to a mutual friend of ours and said I'd love to get hold of good old Gary, and I asked what he was doing. I was told he was working in a theatre up in Windmill Street in London. He was doing Pump Boys and Dinettes with Charlene Carter and Paul Jones from Manfred Mann. To cut a long story short, this guy said he couldn't give me Gary's phone number, but he had his manager's number. I phoned her immediately and told her that I'd been away in Australia for four years and that I was an old pal of Gary's. I left my phone number, and she said she'd pass on the message. Five minutes later, the phone rang, and it was Gary. "Elsie!" He used to call me Elsie. Anyway, he went on, "Oi, Elsie, I'll meet you tonight. I'm doing a show up the West End."

We met in a pub in Windmill Street, and he told me that he was doing all right and was in a TV series called Auf Wiedersehen, Pet. I'd never heard of it, as I'd been on the other side of the world. He said, "Yeah, it's really popular. Prime-time telly!"

Then this older woman joined us, like a Shirley Ann Field, you know, nice nails and bit of a bust and said, "Wayne! Can I have your autograph?" He looked at me, because we both liked older woman and said, "Yeah, all right, darling." He signed his autograph Wayne Holton. I said, "Hey, you're doing all right," and he replied, "Yeah, you don't know the half of it."

He said he was up doing all these Tennent Super Lager adverts on the telly. I was glad he was doing so well because he was a pal, you know.

I said to Gary, "You're doing really well, aren't you? You're on the TV, you're in a West End theatre musical and doing Tennent's adverts. You are doing all right." He said, "Yeah, but I don't half miss the old days." I reckon he would have given it all up to get the band back together. But I said, "Well, too late for that. You fucked up too many times."

It was common knowledge that Gary had a drug problem earlier in his life, but he told the producers of Auf Wiedersehen, Pet it was a thing of the past and that he not only had kicked his drug and alcohol addiction, but he was also considering helping other people who had lost their way and become addicted. There was, however, some media speculation about whether Gary had actually managed to kick his heroin habit during the first series.

FRENCHY : Yes, of course, Gary was never off the stuff. He was using until he died. In the early eighties, he used to pick me up in his yellow Citroen. I remember because my best friend from where I come from in France was a drug addict and had one just like it. What is it with that type of car and drug users? It was a weird coincidence. Anyway, we just used to go and get drunk and stuff.
Lots of people we knew were dying, including Sid (Vicious). It was all shocking, especially when people were starting to have families. I'd already been through it in Crete. I spent a year there and came off heroin, cold turkey, which was like hell. For three months I couldn't sleep, I couldn't eat, I was shaking. It was

really bad. But I actually came off it, and I came back to London in early '76, so I knew how difficult it was. Anyway, Gary and I hung around together. People knew that. But I would like to add that at this point Gary wasn't using that much. It was manageable.

MIKE QUINN : I introduced Gary to a friend of mine, Terry, in Bayswater. There were a lot of bands at Terry's place, and some of them were quite famous, like Killing Joke, who were quite hot at the time. The guys loved Gary and thought he was wonderful. He got well with all of them. I knew Killing Joke from the Reading Festival when I worked there.

Hanging out with someone like Gary was as if you owned the world, and we were all free spirits. I never got into heroin or coke, which they were into. I used to like to smoke weed. But you didn't really think about who was into what at the time, it was all just about partying and having fun. Gary was a real party animal. I never saw him shoot up. That didn't happen, as far as I was aware. He hid it very well. Terry's dead now, but I think back then, he was dealing in a big way, with all the big super-groups. I do remember, when we left, Gary turned to me before he got in the car and said, "That guy's a wizard." He called him a wizard, and I didn't know what he was talking about. I don't know to this day, what it meant.

Gary Holton outside the Piccadilly Theatre 1984

Gary outside the theatre 1984

FAST LIVING

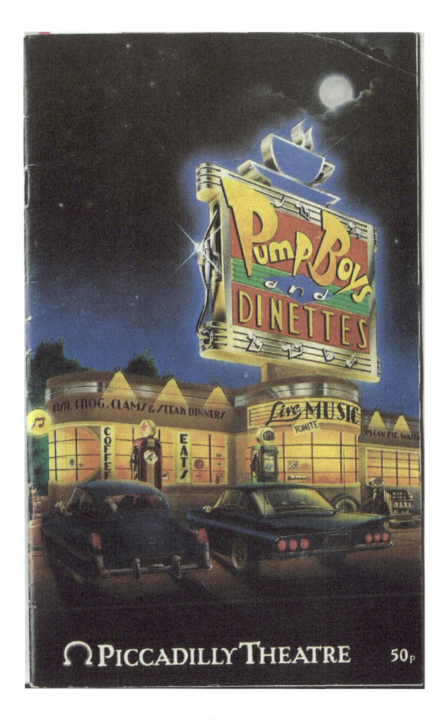

Ω PICCADILLY THEATRE

Denman Street, Piccadilly Circus, London W1
Managing Director Ian B. Albery

BY ARRANGEMENT WITH IAN B. ALBERY
APS LTD IN ASSOCIATION WITH
FREEDMAN PANTER LTD PRESENT

PAUL JONES
KIKI DEE   BRIAN PROTHEROE
GARY HOLTON
CARLENE CARTER   JULIAN LITTMAN

IN

PUMP BOYS AND DINETTES

CONCEIVED AND WRITTEN BY
JOHN FOLEY, MARK HARDWICK,
CASS MORGAN, DEBRA MONK
JOHN SCHIMMEL AND JIM WANN

DIRECTED BY DAVID TAYLOR

PRODUCTION DESIGNED BY TIM GOODCHILD
LIGHTING BY HOWARD EATON
SOUND BY JONATHAN DEANS OF AUTOGRAPH
MUSICAL SUPERVISION BY ROGER WARD
CHOREOGRAPHY BY DOMINI WINTER

First performance at the Piccadilly Theatre 20 September 1984

MIKE QUINN : I feel like I'm telling tales now, talking about this. But it was a different time back then. Drugs in the music scene were normal, and people were openly smoking weed in clubs. Having a joint at the time, wasn't really a big deal. Heroin, however, wasn't something you would want to be known to be doing. It was frowned upon, even back then. And I too frowned upon it.

Gary was living in Maida Vale, and when I was taking him back there that night he said, "Mike, have you got twenty-five quid on you?" I answered, "What do you want it for, Gary?" He wouldn't tell me, but I thought I knew what he wanted it for, so I said, "No, I haven't Gary, and you need to get off that shit!" In fact I was quite annoyed with him, and I didn't think I would be helping him by giving it to him. He was very, very forceful, and I do remember he went on about it. I didn't even know what heroin was at the time, but I knew what coke was. So when Gary asked me for money, I assumed he wanted it for coke, not heroin.

We went back to his flat, and he said I could crash there. I remember going in, and there was a girl there in bed, in one of the rooms. I can't remember how many rooms he had. But he asked this girl to get out of the bed, because I was going to sleep there. We were both a bit pissed, to put it mildly. We'd been drinking and clubbing.

Between filming the TV series, Gary would do commercials and plays, and it was at such a time that he met his old friend and fellow actor, Gary Shail, again.

GARY SHAIL : In 1983 I was approached to play the leading role in a new stage musical called His Master's Voice to be premiered at The Half Moon theatre in London's East End. The play was a parody on the music industry and would require actors who could also sing and play musical instruments. I had a meeting to discuss the role with the producers, who were keen for my involvement due to my recent popularity on TV. The money wasn't very good, so I was a tad hesitant until they told me who was to play my father—Gary Holton!

> "I knew Gary was doing heroin (amongst other things), but it didn't, at this stage, seem to be much of a problem, and he had never tried to get me to do it.
> Except once!"

GARY SHAIL : It was great to see Gary again. He looked fit and well, and his new success as a TV star suited him well. He was still living in Maida Vale but no longer with Donna. He was now living with a stunning long-legged blue-eyed blonde called Sue and had bought a smart two-bedroomed flat in Warwick Avenue (I think?). Gary was also now driving a car, which was great, as he could give me a lift to rehearsals every morning.

Rehearsals were great fun, and we managed to stay relatively clean and sober for most of them, but as soon as the show opened, that all changed. As we no longer had to be up early for rehearsals, Gary left the car at home so he could have a few drinks in the theatre bar after the show. This would inevitably lead us into London's West End, where all the clubs were now available to us (due to our newly acquired celebrity), and we rarely got home, if at all, before light. This pissed Sue off no end, and I'm sure she blamed me, as I wasn't made to feel quite as welcome at their place as I once had been. Eventually, I stopped going round altogether, as I didn't want to create a bad atmosphere.

Gary and I started meeting at the pub before the show, which wasn't such a good idea at all, as sometimes we got so pissed, we could barely stand, let alone sing and act. This never seemed to bother the audience, though, and the show was a critical and financial success. Gary had told me he had seriously thought about giving up singing, but this show (His Master's Voice) had re-ignited his desire to pick up the microphone, and we should get a new band together. I thought it would be suicidal! I knew Gary was doing heroin (amongst other things), but it didn't, at this stage, seem to be much of a problem, and he had never tried to get me to do it. Except once!

FRENCHY : I wanted to do a single with Gary. At one point we had a lot of big bands with big names. Gary told me that he preferred to keep our friendship separate from business, so we never recorded anything with him. I was really good friends with Lemmy as well. I had Hawkwind on my label. Although Lemmy said he would never record with Hawkwind again, I managed to get him back in to Hawkwind to record a track for us.

GARY SHAIL : One night we were in a little pub in Chelsea's King's Road when we were joined by a strange-looking woman, whom Gary knew well. After a few drinks, we went back to her extremely smart flat, where we had some more drinks and some lines of cocaine. She then disappeared briefly then re-appeared carrying a small leather pouch. Inside was a small dirty silver spoon, a length of rubber tubing and a hypodermic needle. All the paraphernalia for mainlining smack! I must admit I was intrigued and more than a little curious, as she also produced a fresh lemon which she proceeded to squeeze a little juice from onto the dirty spoon. She then produced a small bag of brownish powder and poured a little of it into the juice. Using an onyx table lighter, she heated up the mixture before sucking it up into the syringe and flicking the tip of the needle with her perfectly manicured fingernail. I'm not sure if Gary had told her I hadn't done this before, but I was 'buzzing' from the coke and booze, so before I had a chance to think about it, I was stripped to my vest with the rubber tubing tied round my upper arm. I looked at Gary, who just gave me a devilish grin as the strange woman tightened the tourniquet and began slapping my arm to raise a vein.

As soon as the heroin had entered my bloodstream, I could taste it! Then suddenly it felt like someone had poured a bucket of boiling water over my head. Within seconds, I was in a different world. I felt so content and worry-free, you could have told me that you were going to chop off my arms and legs with a rusty axe, and I wouldn't have cared less. Now I knew why Gary loved this drug so much. I never did it again!

FRENCHY : The thing you have to understand is that being a heroin addict was never okay. Even in the music business it was really frowned upon. It wasn't the thing to do. So they had to hide it, basically. They couldn't really tell everyone. It was something they kept to themselves and dealt with the best they could. So there were a few flats and a few places they could go and jack up and be themselves without anybody judging them.

GARY SHAIL : The band The Actors was formed out of necessity rather than design. Due to the popularity of Auf Wiedersehen, Pet, Gary was asked to appear on a television show called The Tube. Transmitted live from the studios in Newcastle, the show, presented by Jools Holland and Paula Yates, had proved popular with music fans in England. It often featured unsigned bands playing live—unlike its BBC predecessor, Top of the Pops, where chart success was a requisite, and miming was the order of the day.

The new band (The Actors) would consist of me on bass and backing vocals, Dave John on drums (Dave was also a well-known actor at the time), Dennis Stratton, who had only recently left Iron Maiden, on guitar, a keyboard player whose name escapes me and Gary Holton, of course, on lead vocals. Gary had already written the song (Long-legged Blue-eyed Blonde) which in retrospect very un-p.c. but even now still makes me giggle.

Joe McGann, who was also the lead singer in my band, was drafted in to manage rehearsals and organise train tickets, expenses, etc. Out of all of us, Joe was definitely the most sensible. I can only remember us having one rehearsal before we all went to the pub. After all, it wasn't rocket science, just good old-fashioned four-four rock 'n' roll. How we got Dennis Stratton still eludes me to this day, but even after a skinful, he was a fucking genius! Putting him and Gary in the same country, let alone on the same stage, was going to be risky, but Joe McGann made us promise to behave ourselves until we had finished the show, and we did.

We all turned up at the train station, on time. We didn't forget anything or abuse our fellow travellers in any way. We arrived at the TV studios on time, were polite to the security men at the gate, did a run-through for the cameras and sound people and then waited patiently in our designated dressing room for the show to start. Paula Yates was on a break from the show at the time and had been replaced by Leslie Ash, who also starred in Quadrophenia, so we all felt very comfortable about Gary's impending interview.

First off, they showed a clip of Auf Wiedersehen, Pet, featuring Gary and Timothy Spall, and then the red light went on for the interview. All was going well until Leslie mentioned Germany, upon which Gary told a story about being seduced by a 'ladyboy' and feeling his/hers bits and bobs. I was pissing myself laughing! This was going out live, for fuck's sake, and it was brilliant! Leslie was bright red and at a loss for words. God knows what the producers thought he might say next. Leslie quickly rounded up the interview, and suddenly we were on. And then we were off and it was all over.

We were invited to stay on for after-show drinks, but Joe, in his wisdom, declined the offer, thinking it safer to get us all on the first available train heading south. So within the hour, we were back at the train station.

FAST LIVING

Gary Shail © The Actors

GARY SHAIL : Unfortunately, it was rush hour on the train, and there weren't enough seats available for us all to sit together. So Joe suggested we move to first class and pay the extra ticket price to the conductor if and when he came to check. So that's what we did. First class was empty, so we made ourselves comfortable before Gary, Dennis and I headed off to find the bar. (Back then, trains had proper bars and not those ridiculous trolley things that always get in the way when you're trying to get off the fucking train!) Once we had located the bar, we bought it! All of the beer we could carry, and as many miniatures of whiskey we could stuff in our pockets were purchased with the rest of the expenses money, and we clanked our way back to first class. After about an hour of serious drinking, Gary fell asleep curled up on his seat, whilst the rest of us stared drunkenly out of the window as the world flashed by. Suddenly, the carriage door was flung open, and a weedy voice demanded, "Tickets please." Gary didn't move! Joe tried to explain the situation and offered to pay the excess fares, but Weed Voice was having none of it, and insisted weedily that we move back to second class.

Gary still didn't move! Joe protested politely, but I could see that Denis was getting wound up and this was going to get messy. Weedy Voice then turned his attention onto Gary, who was still fast asleep. "TAKE YOUR FEET OFF THE SEAT, SON." Dear old Weedy grabbed Gary's legs. Gary came to with a start and quite accidentally kicked poor Weedy in his nether regions. It must have been terrifying for Gary. One minute he was in dreamland and the next confronted by a screaming man in uniform clutching his bollocks. I couldn't stop laughing, which made Wincing Weedy even angrier. He backed out of the carriage stating, "You lot haven't heard the last of this!" and we hadn't!

After about twenty minutes, the train started to slow down. I was sure that the next station was not a scheduled stop, and I was right. As we pulled into Grantham (birthplace of Maggie Thatcher), we could already see the police lining the station platform, and some of them had dogs! Everyone sobered up immediately or at least tried to. Gary, who was now wide awake, suggested going on the offensive. As soon as the train stopped, we hopped off the train, led by Gary, looking as calm and as cheerful as possible.

Gary took complete control of the situation and explained who we were and what had happened. He was so charming and reasonable that even the dogs were mesmerised. The fucker even signed autographs for the police, who then arranged for next train through to make another unscheduled stop to pick us all up. In fact, the train we next got on actually arrived back in London before the one we were originally on. **GENIUS!!!**

There was a club in Maida Vale called The Top Hat and Tails Club, and Gary ran it for a couple of days a week, hoping his newfound fame would bring the punters in.

RONNIE THOMAS : I did see Gary towards the end because I was in London then. I saw him a couple of times. He'd opened up a club in Maida Vale or somewhere, a Top Hat and Tails Club. I went down there with Keith. I was sharing a flat with Keith up in Hampstead, and Gary was living in Maida Vale.

He looked a bit drawn. Towards the end of Auf Wiedersehen, Pet, he didn't look very bonny. I did bump in to him, but he was mixing with a different crowd who were a bit dubious, in my opinion. And he had more money. He was going down to clubs, like Stringfellows. I didn't have that sort of money then.

GLEN MATLOCK : Around about the time of Auf Wiedersehen, Pet, Gary and I had a go at doing a band project together. We did some recordings. It was really good, actually. It was me and Gary and James Stevenson (Chelsea, International Swingers), James Harwell on keyboards and a guy called McIntosh on drums. He used to be the drummer in Doll by Doll. This was when Gary was still doing the TV series. The thing with Gary was that you could never pin him down to things, but we cut three tracks, and EMI were interested.

Funny story—there's a club round here (Maida Vale) called The Top Hat and Tails. It was like a late-night drinking club. Bit low-rank, but a laugh. We all went there one night and got up to high jinks, and everybody crashed out on a sofa. Everybody woke up at half past ten the next morning on the sofa. I said, "Hang on, Gary, we've got a meeting with EMI." And he said, "Come on, let's go!" He used to buy a car for about a hundred and fifty quid, and when he got fed up with it, he would just leave it somewhere. We all jumped in this car, and drove down the Edgware Road. There's one little bit just under the underpass where it goes into the dual carriageway, and there was a fence in the middle of the road.

We were hammering down there, and Gary was driving, although he shouldn't have been. He was really hung over and still drunk, I can imagine, and some bloke tried to overtake him. Gary was having none of it.

FAST LIVING

Well, this guy was just about to overtake, and bear in mind, there was a fence in the middle of the road, and Gary opened the driver's door, so the bloke couldn't get past. We were both going at thirty-five to forty miles per hour. You could hear this bloke in the other car scream, and Gary just laughed.

Chapter 9

The Final Curtain

As the second series of Auf Wiedersehen, Pet started filming in February 1985, Gary found himself with financial problems. He hadn't paid tax since 1979, and he had a large mortgage on his house in Maida Vale, totalling £48,500. Gary had considerable debts and two bankruptcy orders totalling £60,000.

During the filming of both series of Auf Wiedersehen, Pet, he only made two other TV appearances. He appeared in the TV series Minder, where he played the role of the villain, Barry. And he had an unaccredited role as an extra, playing Bernard Scoop in ITV's series Bulman. There was a rumour that Gary was offered the role of Nick Cotton in Eastenders and turned it down. I seriously doubt he would have turned anything down at this point when he was accepting unaccredited roles. The role of Nick Cotton went to Gary's friend, John Altman.

FRENCHY : I think he started to use heavily when the money troubles started. He numbed himself just to forget the shit he was in. But by then, I didn't see him much. In fact, I think I saw him once or twice in 1984, and I was with my wife each time.

In the spring of 1985, the English tabloid newspapers were relentlessly hounding Gary by running exclusive articles about his private life. Gary wanted to start a therapy group to help heroin addicts, and he felt that he wouldn't be taken seriously whilst the newspapers were running articles about his own alleged addiction, which he claimed was a thing of the past. Gary became ever more concerned by the media attention to his private life, which added to his worries about his financial situation.

MAX SPLODGE : Susan is the exact opposite of Donna—really quiet and polite, but she let Gary get away with murder. Gary wasn't really the marrying kind. Of everyone I've ever met, and I've met quite a few in the music business, I've never met anyone quite as hedonistic as him. He was never boring. Sometimes a bit frightening, but never boring.

Gary's response to all the pressure was to not deal with it but to revert to his former habits. If he had never stopped using, then this certainly marked the point where his drug use accelerated. During this time, he was at a low and very vulnerable point. He became paranoid and preferred to hang out with a few people he had just met, and whom were considered very bad for him by his old friends. He preferred the company of a girl he met in a pub. Her name was Jahnet, and she lived with her partner. She in turn instinctively felt Gary needed taking care of. People didn't understand his choices at this time, and Gary wasn't explaining himself at all.

BEN DEL REY : It was late August 1985, and I was at the Notting Hill Carnival. I was dancing in the gardens under the motorway, Portobello Road, when I heard my name, "Moon, Ben!" Someone grabbed me by the waist and spun me around, and it was fucking Gary Holton, of all people. I hadn't seen Gary in four years. He was doing Auf Wiedersehen, Pet in Newark,

Nottingham. So my dear mate, Gary, gave me a kiss on both cheeks. People were looking at us in recognition or interest. We were overjoyed to see each other. It was like an amazing dream. He said, "Come, let me introduce you to the girl I'm with, Jahnet, and her good friend Michel." We all introduced ourselves to the thump of a reggae tune, as we were by the speakers. Suddenly, we were joking, and the conversation was all innuendo and sexually explicit. For example, Jahnet took my leopard-print scarf, which was all that was left of my ex-girlfriend, and stuck it between her legs. She was wearing 505 Levi hot pants, so my scarf slithered like a happy lanyard, in one leg and through and out the other. Then I was supposed to pull, with Gary holding one end and me the other. We could have made music pulling back and forth, as the scarf was the bow, and her privates the instrument.

So we decided to go to my place, which was in the area. We got as far as Organic Planet (health food shop, which Gary called the rabbit shop.) We all cracked up—ha-ha-fucking-ha to funny Gary, saying that, with that Holton body movement and that cockney charm. His voice sounded that like a clapper on a church in Bow. Catch a Falling Cockney Star. Well, it came close to that, as we were walking/dancing back to my place, and suddenly something happened. Now this was to become Gary's first real taste of mania, which left an everlasting mark on the poor guy.

We were mobbed by a group of young girls and guys. They recognised him and started calling his name. We felt safe at first, but then things started getting ugly. They ripped his shirt and it got frightening. They were yelling and trying to pull him in, pulling his hair, which was blue with red specks and looked real good, not as punks had it, but a Holton special—proper hairdresser did it. This was back when you didn't have the police up your arse all the time, like now. You had All Saints Road, which was the front line back then. The police didn't go there, plus if you came across a gang of youths and one of you had a handbag or camera, you could be sure it would be taken from you. That's how it was on the streets then, so you can imagine how scared you could get if you were being mobbed or robbed. But we managed to get away, finally. From that day on, he never stopped mentioning how terrified he was of it happening again.

Anyway, he told me that the TV series Auf Wiedersehen, Pet was the fuel in the rocket that was going to shoot him to stardom. He had no doubt about it, that he was making it big time, as he deserved. He had done the Tennent Beer ads and was doing the necessary stuff. He was going the way Tim Spall did, but he was sure he would be even bigger because of his personality.

He saw Sue around that time because he was giving her money for his child, and quite rightly so. But he wasn't with her. He was practically living with Jahnet by this time.

FRENCHY : Susan was really upset about it all. I mean she was a mum and had two sons. Red being born, to me, was like a kind of turning point. I was sure Gary would quit drugs. I told him I'd been through that, and one day he would have to quit. I told him he had to make a choice—you either come off or you die. There's no other way in this game. I was a bit older than most punks and people of this era, and I'd been through it.

FAST LIVING

JAHNET : I knew Gary Holton during the last few months of his life. He was a product of the punk rock 'n' roll era—sex, drugs and rock 'n' roll. He courted the media, and they brought about his decline. Performers like Gary, who have a special high and fast energy, are often tragic and isolated, seeking a home, yet never really finding it. Gary played with all sorts of drugs. They were a form of escape, and he was surrounded by people who were ready to provide them. He was never a one-drug man, nor was he a one-woman man, and had relationships with quite a few ladies, when we—my partner and I—first met him. We all drank at the same pubs, and that's how I came to know him. I lived in a different world to Gary. I didn't watch TV, and I lived with a semi-retired jazz musician. We moved in a circle of body-workers, healers and psychiatrists. My partner and I had an affair with a French dominatrix, when we met Gary. I was going to be her maid for a few weeks, whilst her own maid was away. She had a place in Mayfair, and Gary thought it was an exciting thing to do. I had just bought a PVC maid's dress to wear, when we got talking in the pub. He told me a bit about his life, about being mobbed by fans, etc. He said he had given up heroin before he started the second series of Auf Wiedersehen, Pet, and he said he had made the mistake of telling the producers of the series about it, and they had become edgy with him.

 The media circus began with the publicity run-up to the filming of the second series of Auf Wiedersehen, Pet. There was a ban on talking to the newspapers about the show. Gary didn't mind being written about—he was used to it. I, however, was a little green about the press, and I didn't take much notice until we went to the club, Stringfellows, together. I ended up being photographed with him and portrayed as the new blonde in Gary's life. Gary used to film in Nottingham throughout the week and went back to London at the weekend. Things were not so good between him and his girlfriend, Sue, so he would stay with us for the weekend.

I loved Gary (people either loved him or hated him), but I was not 'in love' with him. We were really close friends for a short while, and his life was moving so fast, I felt the need to protect him. The media attention grew into a feeding frenzy over the summer, and he and his girlfriend separated. Gary had lost his driver's licence and couldn't drive, so we took him up to Nottingham and picked him up, a couple of times.

The media soon found out that Gary had met someone new called Jahnet and that he had what they referred to as 'a tangled love life'. The tabloids seemed obsessed with unearthing more stories about his private life. Gary travelled to Spain for the on-location filming of the second series of Auf Wiedersehen, Pet, in the autumn of 1985. His manager, John Harwood-Bee, and Jahnet travelled with him. John Harwood-Bee stayed for the first week, and a friend of Gary's from Norway went for the second week, when his manager had to return to London. The cast of Auf Wiedersehen, Pet weren't allowed talk to the press about the series they were making. The press hung around Gary, and Central lifted the media ban for Gary, as long as he didn't talk about the TV series.

JAHNET : Gary asked me to go to Spain with him, because he didn't want to be alone, and Central wanted someone with him. His manager, John Harwood-Bee, and an old friend from Norway also came with us. The atmosphere was very tense whilst filming, and the media

were creeping around. When we returned to the UK, the story broke about Gary's heroin addiction. This was the first time the newspapers wrote about his heroin habit, as the stories before were always about booze and women. He was in a lot of debt, and he knew his career might be over because of all of this. Gary had been ill earlier, something to do with his brain, and he seemed to live his life on the edge, without any real thought for tomorrow.

The tabloid newspaper The Star was promised an interview with Gary when he returned to England, as long as they respected his need for privacy in Spain and not run any more stories about him until he could talk to them. Upon returning to England, Gary found that The Star hadn't respected his privacy and had run a fictitious story about his manager locking Gary up for a month to rid him of his drug addiction.

Gary was furious, and when two reporters from The Star managed to track Gary down at his local pub, where he was waiting for a meeting with his manager, John Harwood-Bee, there was a brief argument. It was no wonder that Gary and a friend didn't welcome the reporters with open arms, and it was alleged that Gary's friend had threatened the reporters and broken their camera.

The next day, The Star ran the headline 'Heroin Hoodlum'. Gary was devastated, and his mother, Joan, fell ill after reading the newspaper, which upset Gary even more. The tabloids were hurting his family, and there was nothing Gary could do about it. He was becoming more difficult to work with on the set of Auf Wiedersehen, Pet, and the pressure was starting to get to him.

MAX SPLODGE : I was living in Kent when he was doing the TV series, and I would go over to Maida Vale to meet up with him. When I saw the first series, I was sure he wasn't taking anything. But in the second series, I think it was apparent that he was. And when I saw him he was acting paranoid. We would normally go out around all these pubs and have a right jolly-up.

Now, suddenly, he didn't want to go. He just wanted to go to this little place. There was a hotel that had a bed and breakfast with a little bar down in the basement. There would never be more than a couple of people staying there, who didn't know who he was, and he would just want to go down there. This would have been after the series got well known. I think this was one of the last times I saw him. He was starting to get pale and have all the symptoms of someone that was using. I've seen it so many times.

I met the girl he was with right at the end. I didn't know a lot about her. That sort of time when he was sloping off…when he was in that bar and he said come over to mine and stay there the night instead of going all the way back to Kent. And I said, "Yeah, all right." And then he said, "Tell you what, maybe we can go round Jahnet's then and have a few beers and that?" I'd heard quite a lot about her, and I didn't really fancy the idea, because I thought we were staying round with Sue.

I let him go off round to Jahnet's, and I think that was pretty much the last time I saw him. This was a point in his life when talking to him was sometimes okay, and other times it wasn't making any sense. It was obvious to me that he was using again, if not, all the time. He kept on about this woman, who apparently lived with her boyfriend, and he didn't mind. He showed me a photo of her. I thought, "What on earth for, when you've got Sue at home?" He said, "Oh, you don't understand, so I'll explain it another time," but he never ever did. It's one of life's mysteries. Sue at home with his kid and his step-kid, Max, and he would go round to this scruffy old flat and sleep on a mattress on the floor with these people he didn't really know. It seemed slightly weird to me.

Gary had been filming the second series the night before his death and returned to London that same day. People who saw him commented on how forlorn and pale he looked. On the evening of the 24th October 1985, Gary and Jahnet arrived at his friend, Paul Witta's, flat.

JAHNET : The night before he died, he was sad and broken. We drove back from Nottingham, and he was due for rehearsals at nine a.m. the following day, in Warwick Avenue. When we arrived back in London, he rushed out for last order at the local pub. We didn't go because we were trying to make him stay in. He came back a lot calmer, having spoken to a reporter he knew. Then, he suddenly wanted to go out again. I couldn't let him go on his own, and I felt I just had to go with him. We went to some friends of his in Wembley. They talked with him for an hour or so, as he was still quite upset. Then we went to sleep on a single bed on the floor. I set the alarm for nine a.m. as he had to go to rehearsals.

When I woke up the next morning, I couldn't arouse him. It frightened me to the point of hysteria. I shouted his name, more and more loudly. I was pretty much hysterical, and the couple we were staying with came in to the room. They tried to help me, as I was sobbing and refused to let go of him. Even when the police came, they couldn't make me get up. I didn't want him to be left alone. I lay next to him for more than an hour, until they finally took him away. Right up until the actual hearing at the Coroner's Court, I really thought he had died of a broken heart. I was confused and very angry when they said he died of a heroin overdose and booze cocktail as his last drink. I hadn't been with him at the pub, but I never saw him shooting up anything. Did he get up whilst I was sleeping? I'll never know. We had often talked about the hidden and secretive world of heroin. He was making a record with Glen Matlock, and there was a special song on it called Sweet Soul Injection, which included the lyrics, "See me through to the bitter end..." and I did. Even now I can't believe he died of a heroin overdose. It certainly wasn't suicide. I'm very sure of that.

When a death is suspected to have been either sudden with unknown cause, violent, or unnatural, a coroner decides whether to hold a post-mortem examination and, if necessary, an inquest. The inquest into Gary's death was held on 19th December 1985 at the Coroner's Court in Hornsey, North London and left many unanswered questions.

BEN DEL REY : I'd been dabbling in drugs, and Gary Holton helped me get clean. I left and went on a trip with Barry Jones (guitarist for The London Cowboys, and Johnny Thunders, co-owner of famed early punk club in London 'The Roxy'). When I got back, Gary helped me out by putting me into acting school to help my career.

I was very upset by Gary's death. I should have been there. I know what to do when someone turns blue.

FAST LIVING

Gary didn't kill himself nor did anyone else. It was all just such a dreadful thing to happen to my dear friend.

The autopsy report states that Gary died from an overdose of alcohol and morphine and that he had traces of diazepam and cannabis in his system. Pathologist Dr Rufus Crompton said that Gary would have been drinking less than half an hour before his death and that the morphine would have made him unconscious within a matter of minutes. His blood alcohol level was 199mg/dl, and the morphine level was 0.8mg per litre.

If we look more closely at what these findings mean, then 199mg alcohol per dl blood would have resulted in poor judgement, a labile mood and bad muscle coordination (Ataxia). 80–199 mg/dl is regarded as binge drinking, and Gary's blood showed that he was right at the top of the scale. To put it in layman's terms, Gary was pretty pissed that night. Blood alcohol levels over 200mg/dl would have made him throw up and perhaps pass out. To get from 199 ml/dl to 200ml/dl would have represented a small amount of alcohol, a mouthful of brandy perhaps. So you can see how drunk Gary must have been.

A morphine level of 0.8 mg per litre is extremely high (0,5 mg per litre is considered fatal). The medical term for heroin is diamorphine, which is why it was referred to as morphine in the autopsy report. So Gary died of an overdose of alcohol and heroin. In addition, traces of diazepam (valium) and cannabis were found in his system. Diamorphine (heroin) cannot be taken orally and would have had to have been injected. However, no drug equipment was found in the flat where Gary died. Given that Gary was extremely drunk, had taken valium and smoked a spiff, it's incredible he managed to inject himself with heroin at all.

After twice recalling Jahnet to face searching questions, the coroner, Dr David Paul, said, "It must follow from the medical evidence that this man had a fix of heroin. The absence of any evidence to indicate when this was taken and the absence of evidence about finding a syringe and other material for drug abuse leaves enormous unanswered questions. Initially, this was perfectly straightforward. A man who has been a heroin abuser under stress took a fix that proved to be fatal. There is no evidence at all to support a finding that this death is due to misadventure. The gaps in evidence leave me to record the only possible finding in this matter." The coroner, Dr David Paul, recorded an open verdict.

An open verdict in an inquest is when the coroner decides that the evidence is insufficient to deliver one of the specific verdicts: natural causes, unlawful killing, suicide, accidental death or death due to industrial disease. However, if new evidence becomes available at any time, the inquest can be re-opened.

All of the above-mentioned verdicts have to be established to the test within the balance of probabilities, except for suicide and unlawful killing, which have to be proved beyond reasonable doubt. The coroner, Dr David Paul, stated there was no evidence in the flat of any equipment to administer drugs, such as syringes or other material you would expect to find when someone overdoses and becomes unconscious within minutes of administering the drug. So if the court decided there was a reasonable doubt about what had happened the night Gary passed away, there was no evidence to prove it, and therefore, an open verdict was recorded so that it could be opened up again should new evidence or newer technology lead to the need for further inspection into what happened that night.

What really happened on the night he died is still a mystery, and no one has come forward with any new evidence to close the inquiry into his death, which has been an open case for almost thirty years.

So what happened that night? Was it a mistake? Was Gary so drunk that he took the wrong dose of heroin by accident? Or did he in fact take the right dose, not knowing that the heroin he had been given was much more pure than his usual stuff, perhaps? Did he feel so depressed, he decided to end his life just as he was becoming everything that he had always wanted to be? If he did take the heroin whilst at the flat with his friends, why was no drug equipment found in the flat? Could the pathologist have missed something and got it wrong? There are countless unanswered questions.

Gary died halfway through the filming of the second series of Auf Wiedersehen, Pet, but the producers used body doubles and clever editing of dialogue already recorded to allow the series to be completed. The final episode of the second series was broadcast after Gary's death and was dedicated to him.

Gary's funeral was held at Golders Green Crematorium and was attended by friends and family. His father and two brothers, who wept openly as his coffin arrived, supported Gary's mother who collapsed with grief. The coffin was adorned by a huge floral guitar and Gary's co-stars from Auf Wiedersehen, Pet—Jimmy Nail, Tim Healy, Timothy Spall, Kevin Whately, Pat Roach and Christopher Fairbank—attended the funeral and paid their last respects to their friend.

FAST LIVING

FRENCHY : I will never forget Gary, but I'd rather forget how he died.

GARY SHAIL : Phrases such as 'a one-off' and 'they don't make 'em like that anymore' definitely apply to Gary Holton. Not only was he (in my opinion) a massive talent, he was a complex and sensitive man who lived his life at full throttle. I've heard in some quarters that Gary didn't give a fuck or care. But that wasn't the bloke I knew. Gary cared about everything. Probably too much!

MIKE QUINN : Gary gave me a record once. It had a star on it, and he wanted me to have it. It was called Catch a Falling Star. We were in the Warrington Pub in Maida Vale, and Gary introduced me to the singer in the band Mud, and he gave me the record. It was shaped like a star. I remember Gary with great affection, and I was very sad to hear that he died. I had great love for Gary, as a bloke. He was fantastic.

RONNIE THOMAS : Dear Gary had that same thing going for him as Gene Vincent, Iggy Pop and Jim Morrison, that is—he looked like a dude that you could catch crabs off. Plus he had two-hundred-percent charisma, the perfect frontman. I wish he was still here. Drugs are bad for you.

JAHNET : Just like many talents that leave this life early and go to the beyond, no one will ever know how or why they go so early or why in Gary's case they leave us so tragically. When Gary left this life, my world, and the rest of the world, lost a shining light and a being of love. He had so much more to offer. He continues to inspire, and he is greatly missed.

KEITH BOYCE : **The times I spent with Gary are some of the best of my life. Not only was he very sharp, witty and extremely funny, but he was also the best frontman I have ever worked with, and I'd go as far as to say he was one of the greatest frontmen the world has seen.**

I am proud to have been his friend and to have shared such great times on and off stage with him.

Gary lived fast and died young. There were very few red lights or warning signals in his life. If he wanted to do something, he did it without hesitation. For those of us who have been lucky enough to have known Gary, we take his memory with us into the future. He was such a fun person to be with. He was also a kind and caring person and is deeply missed.

FAST LIVING

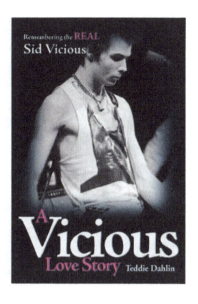

Teddie was 16 years old in 1977, when she was asked to be the translator for the Norway leg of The Sex Pistols Scandinavian tour. The book tells the inside story of the romance between Teddie and Sid Vicious. Instead of the self-destructive caricature of popular myth, Teddie reveals a troubled, vulnerable and generous young man. She gives a first-hand account of four young men at the eye of an international media storm, labouring under the sudden weight of expectation at the height of their fame. We are given a closer look into the dynamics between all the band members and their associates. The last chapters are written in part by Eileen Polk (ex-girlfriend of DeeDee Ramone) and Peter Gravelle, who were in New York at the time of Sid's death.

FAST LIVING

When Tiger Edwards, bass player for the rock band, The Sticks, is found dead of an overdose of alcohol and heroin after a sold out concert, everyone is shocked. Tiger had been clean of drugs for over thirty years. At first, it looks like an accident, or suicide perhaps, but things are not always as they seem. When the police confirm that they found no drug equipment in the room you would expect to find when someone overdoses and dies, the death becomes even more mystifying. Charlotte Hart gets a chance assignment with Melody magazine, which introduces her to the sex, drugs, and rock and roll world of the music business and plunges her into a murder mystery that have left the police baffled. Join Charlie and the colourful array of characters she meets, as together they try to solve the mystery of Tiger's death. Charlie's suburban life changes to one filled with aging rock stars, a handsome bodyguard, a punk-rock grandma, and the obnoxious Sticks manager, who's 'helping' the London Metropolitan Police, Yew Tree Investigation with their inquiries into alleged sexual activities with underage girls. Charlie finds herself digging into a history of crime that goes back more than thirty years. The story has moments of comedy and tragedy that will leave you laughing and crying, but most of all wondering: who killed Tiger and why?

Crime/fiction, first in the Charlie Hart Crime series

Project Polina

As the daughter of a mega-wealthy Russian oligarch, you would assume Polina Averyanov has everything money can buy. When eighteen-year-old Polina aspires to be a pop star, her wealthy father does what any well to do magnate would—he does his best to make his daughter's dream come true and starts Project Polina, but quickly discovers pop stardom cannot be easily bought.

When Polina competes in a small song contest in the Ukraine, her existence comes to the attention of her father's worst enemy, Boris Korzhakov. Boris has reached the higher echelons of Russian politics to head the FSB, which is concerned with internal security of the Russian State, but is also involved in the fight against espionage and organised crime, formerly a faction of the KGB. Boris Korzhakov was Stanislav Averyanov's business partner until Averyanov was arrested for crimes against the state. After bribing his way out of prison, Averyanov moved the major part of his assets to London, without a second thought of his partner's share.

Polina's career isn't taking off, and when there's a direct threat to the Averyanov family, Gresham CPC Global are called in to protect the spoilt young girl. Brody McCaine and his partner, Glen, are asked to guard the girl on a twenty-four-hour basis. Her parents try to work out what they need to do to stay safe, after an arrest order is issued for Stanislav and his assets that remained in Russia, seized by the state. Project Polina suddenly changes from making her a pop star to keeping her alive.

Charlotte Hart is still living with her dysfunctional family and struggling to make a career for herself as a music journalist while divorcing her husband, who is making life difficult for her. It isn't made any easier by Grandma Blue and her best friend, Doris, who are pushing Charlie into the arms of Doris's divorced grandson, Robert, whom she had a schoolgirl crush on, disregarding the fact that Charlotte and Brody have become close.

It all comes to a head when Brody and Glen turn up at Charlotte Hart's family home, in need of a safe house. Brody's feelings for Charlie become evident to Polina, who has developed a deep crush, bordering on obsession, for Brody. Charlie's dysfunctional family finds itself in the middle of a bitter feud that has international implications and isn't helped by the fact that the band The Sticks road manager, Digger, turns up with problems of his own.

Loyalties are tested as the need to escape from the Hart family house, which is surrounded by FCB agents, becomes imperative. Polina has to leave, or they will all die.

The second book in the Charlie Hart crime series will be released in spring 2014.

About the Author

Teddie Dahlin lives in Oslo, Norway and in addition to writing books, is a freelance music journalist and has written a string of interviews and articles in the UK. Fast Living is her second book.

FAST LIVING

FAST LIVING